Your Next
Great Stock

Your Next Great Stock

How to Screen the Market for Tomorrow's Top Performers

Jack Hough

John Wiley & Sons, Inc.

Published by John Wiley & Sons, Inc., Hoboken, New Jersey.
Published simultaneously in Canada.

Wiley Bicentennial Logo: Richard J. Pacifico

For general information on our other products and services or for technical support, please contact our Customer Care Department within the United States at (800) 762-2974, outside the United States at (317) 572-3993 or fax (317) 572-4002.

Wiley also publishes its books in a variety of electronic formats. Some content that appears in print may not be available in electronic formats. For more information about Wiley products, visit our Web site at www.wiley.com.

Library of Congress Cataloging-in-Publication Data

Hough, Jack, 1972–
    Your next great stock : how to screen the market for tomorrow's top performers / Jack Hough.
        p. cm.
        ISBN 978-0-470-11793-4 (cloth)
    1. Stocks   2. Investments.   I. Title.
    HG4661 .H67   2007
    332.63'2042—dc22
                                                            2007013691

Printed in the United States of America

10 9 8 7 6 5 4 3 2 1

Contents

Introduction

O ver the next year, more than 100 stocks will double in price. Several hundred will produce gains of 50 percent or more. A tiny few stocks will soar fivefold in value.

Those are estimates, of course; they assume the next year will be an ordinary one for stocks. It may not. Perhaps only 40 stocks will double in price, or perhaps even fewer. Still, a small number of stocks will produce enviable returns.

I say "a small number" because there are a vast number of stocks to choose from. These figures are based on a survey of the 6,000 or so stocks listed on the big three U.S. trading venues: The New York Stock Exchange, the American Stock Exchange, and the Nasdaq. If we look at smaller venues and foreign exchanges, too, the list expands to more than 30,000 stocks.

This book is about finding stocks that are poised to become the market's next big gainers. It's more a detective manual than an investment book. You'll be able to find these companies because they've already left clues. The clues aren't much more complicated than the mustard stains and shoe scuffs Sherlock Holmes relied on. But whereas those clues told

Holmes where a suspect had been, you'll use clues that tell you where companies are going.

One company's clue might be a slight quickening in its sales growth. Another's clue might be that its managers have suddenly started buying its shares. Still another company might look ripe for a takeover judging by the metrics that merger-and-acquisition experts use.

The best way to search for particular clues—the only way to perform a thorough search, in fact—is through something called *stock screening*. Stock screening involves using software to quickly scan a large database of information. Too many investors use a less-methodical, company-by-company approach to stock investing. They wait to hear about "must-own" stocks from co-workers and television pundits. Then they focus too much of their research on stories others are telling about those companies rather than studying the clues. By using that approach, these investors aren't giving themselves a fair shot at finding big gainers, for a few reasons. They're hearing mostly about stocks that have already become popular and have produced their biggest gains. They're relying more on opinion than evidence. And they're limiting their exposure to just a few stocks.

Suppose it takes you an hour to do basic research on one company. Suppose, too, that you love researching stocks like a grade-schooler loves potty jokes—you decide to make it a 40-hour-a-week job. At that pace, it would take you three years to get to all of the aforementioned 6,000 stocks. By that time, of course, your research would be out of date. You'd be forced to start over.

Stock-screening software allows you to size up thousands of stocks in seconds. It doesn't pick stocks for you. It simply searches for the clues you specify to reduce, say, a 6,000-company database to a dozen or so prime suspects. That allows you to focus your research time on the companies most likely to produce sizable gains. Of course, whether you end up with the right companies depends on whether you start with the right mix of clues. This book will see to that.

It might sound sensationalistic to say this book is about finding the market's next big gainers—stocks that could double your money in a couple of years. The broad stock market, after all, has returned an average of about 10 percent a year over the past century. Even the most successful money managers have outperformed the market by only a few percentage points a year over long time periods. Why should you try to do better? And, who am I to claim this book will show you how?

Let me answer the second question first. Think of me as your own personal thief and reporter. As part of my job writing about stock screening for *SmartMoney* magazine, SmartMoney.com, and the *Wall Street Journal*, I steal. I take nearly all of my ideas from leading researchers and the world's most successful investors. Then I report back to readers with the loot. For this book, I've cherry-picked the best of what I've stolen and packed it into one guide.

As to whether it's okay for us as level-headed investors to go after sensational stock gains, I'll defer to one of the people I'll be stealing from shortly. As manager of the Fidelity Magellan mutual fund, Peter Lynch sought and captured returns so large he developed a new terminology to discuss them. A *ten-bagger* for Lynch is a stock that increases tenfold in value, and he found many. (Magellan itself was a 28-bagger during his 13 years at the helm, meaning it turned $10,000 investments into more than $280,000.) In a recent *SmartMoney* interview, Lynch said he focuses only on stocks he thinks can double or triple his money in a couple of years. "That's what I need to make up for my mistakes," he said.

This book is a hunt for Lynch's ten-baggers. It won't show you how to allocate your assets among stocks, bonds, real estate, cash, and other holdings, although you should take the time to learn that elsewhere. It won't tell you how to develop a long-term savings plan, although that's important to know, too. It's simply about going after stock returns large enough to more than make up for your mistakes.

Before I start reading an investment book, I like to know who it's for, what I'll learn, and how long it will take. This book is for anyone who buys stocks or wants to. It won't require math skills beyond some quick arithmetic, and it will provide the background investment knowledge you'll need along the way. The book contains about 75,000 words. If you read at an average pace (about 250 words a minute) it will take you five hours to finish. Let's look at what you'll cover during those five hours.

Part One: Your Next Great Stock

If you're wondering whether it's possible to beat the stock market or whether you should try, this section will provide the answers.

Chapter 1 explains why you should own stocks, no matter how high savings account rates are at your bank or how much the neighbor's house has increased in value since he bought it.

Chapter 2 is a quick walk through more than 100 years of stock-picking theory. It starts with mathematicians who created a better way to gamble on cards and dice. It then shows how economists tried to apply this gambling math to the stock market to show that stock-picking doesn't work. It covers the stunning rise of the index mutual fund industry. Then it details how recent evidence overwhelmingly suggests those early math models were flawed, and why it's a better time than ever for stock picking.

Chapter 3 covers something you're probably wondering by now: If these stock-picking strategies work so well, how come they haven't been used up by stock pickers? The answer has to do with decision-making skills we've inherited from our shorter, hairier ancestors. I'm not talking about your Grandpa Ernie.

Chapter 4 tells you why stock screening is the best way to find stocks. It also explains why you're probably the best stock picker you know. Don't blush. Wait until you read just how useless those tips from stockbrokers, pundits, mutual fund managers, and even friends and relatives probably are.

Chapter 5 is all about risk and reward. I know stock picking sounds risky. It's less risky than the alternatives, and I'll explain why. I'll also explain why the mutual fund industry has spent oodles over the past 50 years to convince you that you don't know a good business when you see one.

Chapter 6 shows you how to tell a great stock-picking strategy from a lousy one. There are five things your strategies must have, and impressive past performance is only one of them.

Part Two: Tools and Clues

Here you'll learn about what's in that mountain of information you're going to screen through, and which tools are best for the job.

Chapter 7 describes how to run a stock screen. It's short. No one likes instruction manuals, and with a good stock screener you won't need one.

Chapter 8 introduces the screeners. I'll only cover good ones that are either free or cheap. I have a bias, because at the time of this writing I also write stories for one of the companies whose screeners I'll review. But I'll be as fair as a priest judging a pie contest when I compare the features.

Chapter 9 explains where the numbers come from. If financial statements are foreign to you (and not just the foreign ones), this chapter will help you read them. It's short, too.

Chapter 10 details things you can screen for. If financial statements contain the raw ingredients, these metrics are the baked goods. If you don't know your *return on equity* from your *free cash flow*, this chapter will fix that. It will also provide tips on how to best use each piece of information.

Part Three: Strategies

This is where you'll make money. I've collected 15 of the most powerful stock-screening strategies I've found. Most come from the kind of leading-edge market researchers who advise hedge funds and institutions on their stock-picking methods. All the strategies are backed up with concrete evidence that shows they work. A few are designed to mimic market-crushing money managers like Warren Buffet and Peter Lynch.

Chapter 11 starts you off with tips on how best to use the screening strategies. You'll learn why faithfulness to a single strategy is overrated, and why the debate over whether you should search for *growth* stocks or *value* stocks is largely pointless.

Chapter 12 introduces the *Buy High, Sell Higher* screen. Find out why share price momentum is one of the best predictors of higher stock prices, but only if you look for it the right way.

Chapter 13 features the *Impatient Value* screen. See how to search for stocks that are priced to pay off over the next five years, but that just might do so over the next several months.

Chapter 14 looks at the *Surprise, Surprise* screen. Learn why positive earnings surprises tend to foretell big stock gains, particularly when paired with another surprise.

Chapter 15 covers the *Tomorrow's Breakthroughs* screen. I'll explain how you can use the dollars companies are spending on research today to predict tomorrow's profits and stock gains.

Chapter 16 details the *New Dogs* screen. It improves upon one of the most successful dividend-based stock strategies of all time.

Chapter 17 discusses the *Bold Is Beautiful* screen. Analysts who stray far from their peers when forecasting earnings take big risks. Often, they have good reason to do so. Find out how to profit from their moxie.

Chapter 18 presents the *Rising Expectations* screen. By the time you get to it you'll have learned that Wall Street's buy and sell recommendations aren't much use to stock pickers. This screen shows how to vastly improve the predictive power of analysts' research.

Chapter 19 describes the *Follow the Leaders* screen. When a company's bosses buy its shares, there's a good chance the stock price is headed significantly higher. You'll see how to tell which purchases are mostly likely to predict big gains.

Chapter 20 looks at the *Accrual to be Kind* screen. By looking for companies that are generating more cash profits than paper profits, you can find winners. This chapter will show you how.

Chapter 21 features the *Sales on Sale* screen. Learn why one of the simplest measures of whether a stock is cheap is also one of the best.

Chapter 22 covers the *Combination Platter* screen. It starts with companies with low share prices and plenty of valuable assets. Then it searches for no less than nine other promising clues that have historically produced astounding returns.

Chapter 23 presents *guru* screens. See how to put the market-beating strategies of some of the world's greatest investors to work in your portfolio.

Part Four: Your Next Great Stock, Revisited

Here you'll learn what to do with that handful of stock-screen survivors you've just produced.

Chapter 24 shows you how to research your screen survivors to decide which ones to buy.

Chapter 25 offers some thoughts on knowing when to sell.

One more thing: I've built some online screens that you can run for free. They're based on some of the strategies covered in this book. You'll find them at YourNextGreatStock.com.

Part One

YOUR NEXT GREAT STOCK

Chapter 1

You Should Own Stocks

You probably already know this. After all, you're reading a book called *Your Next Great Stock*. But you should own stocks.

There's nothing abstract or exotic about a stock. It's simply a piece of a business. Stocks are born when companies sell shares of themselves to investors. Sometimes they do this because the original business owners want to cash in part of their stake. Sometimes companies issue shares because they want to raise money for expansion.

Many stocks trade freely among investors after they're issued. Their prices are determined by investor demand, which is, in turn, determined by how valuable investors think these businesses are or will become.

If you own stocks, you own businesses. If you pick good businesses—ones that grow and become more valuable—the price of your stocks will rise. Your businesses might also distribute part of their profits to you in cash. They might make big, one-time distributions when the opportunity arises or little, periodic ones, in fairly regular amounts. These payments are called *dividends*. The combination of share price increases and dividend payments make up, for the most part, the total return you receive from your stocks. The purpose of this book is to show you how to find businesses that are likely to produce large total returns.

Owning stocks, even ones that produce average returns, is the best way to build wealth over long time periods.

I know; right now seems like an uncertain time to buy stocks. There's that scandal in the news about the boss who stole money and made his stock price plummet. There's that big economic report due out tomorrow—something about interest rates—that will show whether we're okay. Also, over the past year the stock market (1) fell, so it might keep falling, (2) rose, so it might be expensive, or (3) did nothing, while everyone else got rich in real estate. Plus, the guy on the financial channel who's reporting live from the floor of the stock exchange seems particularly frantic today.

That's what it always looks like.

That boss who stole money is an exception among thousands of honest bosses who can grow your businesses. Whether they want to or not, bosses leave clues as to how reliable they are in their financial reports. We'll see how to find those clues later.

There's a big economic report every day. Ignore them. The reports can't tell you how the stock market will react to the reports. Sometimes the market goes up on miserable news because investors were expecting worse news. Sometimes it goes up because the news is so miserable it causes everyone to figure that someone in charge will finally do something to fix things. You can't use economic news to predict the market's short-term performance, and there's no need to predict the market's long-term performance. Spoiler alert: It's going up.

I'm confident that stock prices will increase significantly over the next 20 years and that stocks will outperform other investments such as bonds, gold, and real estate. I base that belief on two things: past performance and logic. (The importance of using both past performance and logic when developing stock-picking strategies will be made clear later in the book.)

First, the past performance. You've no doubt already seen "Stocks, Bonds, Bills, and Inflation." It's something of a celebrity as financial charts go. Ibbotson Associates, the chart's publisher, will sell you a laminated copy, but there's no need to buy one. Tell a stockbroker you're wavering on whether to renew a big Treasury bond or certificate of deposit that just matured. He'll whip out a copy like he's showing off a picture of his kids.

The chart shows what a single dollar placed in various investments has turned into since 1925. Small-company stocks and large-company stocks are represented by two squiggly lines that soar above the others, turning their dollar bills into numbers so large they look like misprints: $13,706 and $2,658, respectively, by the end of 2006. Two smoother lines representing government bonds and their shorter-term siblings, bills, creep to just $71 and $18. That's barely enough to outpace inflation, the chart's fifth line, which rises to $11. Inflation is the gradual increase in the prices of ordinary goods, everything from a can of beer to a pottery class to an ear exam. If your wealth isn't growing faster than inflation, you're getting poorer.

Look closely at such a chart and you can see what surely must have been scary times for investors: a huge dip in 1929, a long lull in the late 1960s and early 1970s, and a stumble in 2000. Stand further back, though, and you'll see that through war, peace, breakthroughs, and setbacks, stocks have climbed. Buy a large basket of stocks, hold them for a long time, and you'll grow rich. In fact, over long time periods stock returns are remarkably consistent. After inflation, they return about seven percent a year. One study by Wharton professor Jeremy Siegel, for example, found that after-inflation returns averaged 7.0 percent over nearly seven decades ending 1870, then 6.6 percent through 1925 and then 6.9 percent through 2004.

Of course, most people don't have 70 or 80 years to watch their money grow. Those who are approaching retirement might have far fewer. Your stockbroker no doubt has a chart for that, too. It likely consists of three simple pie charts. The first illustrates how if you had held stocks for a single year picked at random between 1925 and 2005, there's a 71 percent chance you would have made money. The second shows that if it was a random five-year period instead of a single year, your chances improve to 87 percent. The final pie chart is one solid color; the market has gone up during every 15-year period since 1925.

Like bonds, real estate is unlikely to outperform stocks over the next 20 years. Yes, I know that your neighbor bought a Long Island bait shack as an investment property a few years back and just sold it for $600,000 as a summer bungalow. But that's a historical exception. The average long-term return of real estate, after subtracting for inflation, might surprise you. It is about zero. According to Yale economist Robert Shiller, houses have returned an average of 0.4 percent a year after inflation since 1890. Nearly all of the positive returns come from two periods: one following World War II and another after 2000. Both periods benefited from artificial boosts to demand. During the first, the government began in earnest to provide subsidized mortgages. During the second, the Federal Reserve slashed interest rates.

The ratio of median house prices to median rents has now more than doubled since World War II, whereas the ratio of share prices to yearly company earnings is pretty close to its World War II level and historical average. That suggests real estate has become far pricier than stocks. Of course, over long time periods, professional real estate investors know how to use enormous leverage to turn skimpy returns into bigger ones. But stock investors can achieve big returns without borrowing money. And stocks are less costly to own: As they say, they never call you in the middle of the night with a leaky toilet. If you get a call like that from your stocks, it's probably a prank.

Perhaps you've seen a late-night infomercial or magazine ad touting the blazing returns of gold. A dollar invested in gold in 1925 grew to just under $31 by the end of 2006. That's more than short-term government bonds returned but less than long-term ones did, and it's a pittance next to stock returns.

"The numbers don't lie," people sometimes say. On Wall Street, as we'll see later in this book, the numbers *do* lie—and they lie often. Past returns are never reason enough to follow an investment strategy, because sometimes they're a fluke and sometimes people manipulate them. Always look for a logical explanation for past returns. The stock strategies contained in this book are based on both strong past returns and reasonable explanations. We'll call those *correlation* and *cause* later. Let's get into the habit of pairing the two now. Without knowing what caused Ibbotson's charts to look the way they do, there's no way to predict whether updated versions 20 years from now will tell the same story.

Companies prosper only to the extent that they can earn positive returns on their resources. A deli that fills $5 sandwiches with $6 worth of pastrami won't stay in business for long. Among the materials most companies use are money, real estate, and raw materials.

Companies that need money often borrow it by issuing bonds to investors. They pay interest on those bonds. That interest represents the cost of their money. Companies pay this cost only because they're confident they can produce profits that exceed it. Stocks outperform bonds over long time periods because companies generate profits that exceed bond interest.

Most companies own or lease real estate. Even Internet companies usually have a headquarters or warehouse. They pay for real estate only to the extent they can use that real estate profitably. Stocks outperform real estate over long time periods because companies produce profits that surpass real estate costs.

Some companies use raw materials to manufacture goods. These materials are called *commodities*. A commodity is a good that's interchangeable with other goods of the same type. Gold is an example. Provided the chemical compositions are the same, one nugget of gold is no better or worse than another of the same size, just as one barrel of oil is the same as the next. Companies wouldn't pay more for raw materials than they can earn by using those materials. Stocks beat gold over long time periods because companies produce profits that are bigger than commodity costs.

Stocks entitle you to a share of a company's money, real estate, and commodities, but that's not what makes them so valuable. Shareholder wealth is created by the people who turn those resources into profits. When you buy stocks, you effectively hire smart people who spend their days figuring out how to make you money. Bonds, houses, and gold can't do that.

So you should own stocks. Chances are, you should put a portion of your money in bonds, real estate, and commodities, too, even though the long-term returns on those investments won't be as good. That's because if stocks have a lousy year, your other investments might have a good one. It keeps returns smoother over time. Mixing different assets together is called *diversification* or *asset allocation* and is outside the scope of this book. Financial planners often tell old investors to favor bonds and young ones to load up on stocks, but what matters isn't so much your age as how much of your savings you'll have to spend over the next decade or two. If you are 35 and adding to rather than spending down your savings, you should load up on stocks. If you are 90 and spend only 1 percent of your saving a year, you should load up on stocks, too. If you are 65 and supplementing a pension by spending 20 percent of your savings each year, you'd better sacrifice some of the higher returns stocks provide for the short-term principal protection you can get in Treasury bills and money market accounts. One type of person shouldn't own stocks at all. Ironically, this type of person seems most likely to ask me which stocks to buy. The person will say, "I've got some money that just freed up and I won't need it for six months. Which stocks should I buy?" To make stock returns work for you, you have to buy good ones and hold them for long time periods. Think short-term, by all means. There's little reason to buy a stock that you don't think can produce enormous returns over the next six months. But don't buy it with the intention of selling it in six months. Give yourself more time to be right.

Oh, and don't worry about the frantic guy reporting from the stock exchange floor. He always sounds like that. He was hired, in part, because be does a great frantic voice, even on ho–hum trading days. That keeps people who own stocks watching television.

Before we continue, I want to make sure your bank hasn't succeeded in confusing you about the difference between investment classes (stocks, bonds, CDs), investment accounts (individual retirement accounts, or IRAs), investment brokers (Charles Schwab), and investment products (mutual funds). If you've ever asked, "Should I buy a stock or an IRA?" your bank has succeeded. The banker probably did that by telling you that the bank has a 5 percent IRA. What the banker means is that the bank offers IRA accounts, and if you put money in one you can buy a CD with that money if you like, and the bank's CDs yield 5 percent. IRAs themselves don't pay anything. They're accounts, not investments.

You can buy stocks in many different accounts: regular brokerage accounts, retirement accounts, college savings accounts, and so on. Some of these accounts carry tax advantages, usually because they're designed to fund something the government wants you to be able to pay for, such as education or retirement. Choosing among account types is important and plenty of books can help you with that choice, but this one is about finding great stocks, not deciding where to put them.

You can buy stocks from many different brokers, ranging from expensive ones that recommend particular investments to cheap ones that just execute your buy and sell orders. To make matters more confusing, the term *broker* can refer to the firm or to a person who works for that firm and either makes recommendations or assists you with placing trades. I recommend you use cheap brokers, sometimes called *discount brokers*. In Chapter 4, I'll explain why the expensive brokers often recommend lousy investments. Cheap brokers generally charge $5 to $15 per stock trade. Choose one based on the annual quality rankings that run in financial publications such as *Barron's* and *SmartMoney* magazine.

You can buy individual stocks or shares of an investment product, such as a mutual fund, that holds them for you. (Some mutual funds hold other investments such as bonds or a mix of investments.) *Actively managed* funds have a fund manager who picks stocks. *Index funds* mimic stock indexes, or baskets of stocks designed to reflect the broad performance of a class of stocks or of the entire market. In other words, actively managed funds try to beat the market, while index funds try to merely match it. I don't recommend letting fund managers pick stocks for you. You'll see why shortly.

That leaves index funds. Many of these are good, cheap investments. You should pick individual stocks instead of or in addition to index funds, though, if you can consistently beat the broad market's returns. You'll find a hint as to whether that's possible in the title of the next chapter.

Chapter 2

You Can Beat the Stock Market

S tock picking is becoming rarer everywhere in the world. Indexing, the opposite of stock picking, is becoming more popular. Stock picking is the act of choosing stocks that look likely to produce better returns than the overall stock market. Indexing refers to buying large baskets of stocks designed to track, but not beat, the market.

It might seem as though stock picking is as popular as ever. Wall Street firms issue regular recommendations on which stocks you should "buy," "sell" and "hold." Pundits argue over whether Google is headed higher or Intel is due for a comeback. James Cramer of CNBC's *Mad Money* bites the heads off of toy bulls and throws chairs around the set while delivering dozens of stock picks each night. But those are anecdotal examples. The flow of investor money tells a different story.

The most popular stock index by far is the S&P 500. Loosely speaking, it tracks the performance of America's 500 largest companies ranked by *market value*. A company's market value is the amount it would cost you to buy the entire company by purchasing all of its shares. The S&P 500 itself isn't an investment. Investors track its movements to get an idea of what the overall stock market is doing. Many index mutual funds are set up to mimic the S&P 500. At the end of 2005, these S&P 500 funds held $1.26 trillion in assets, according to Standard & Poor's, which owns the index (and charges licensing fees to mutual funds that mimic it). That's just over $200 for every person on Earth. It's also a 28-fold increase since 1983.

The world's largest and oldest index mutual fund, the Vanguard 500, started with $11 million in 1976. Today it holds more than 10,000 times that amount in S&P 500–based assets.

The huge flow of money into index funds suggests an increasing number of investors don't believe it is possible to beat the stock market by picking stocks. Or at least, they don't believe they're capable of doing it.

An Indiana University finance professor and one of his graduate students recently set out to create a scorecard—stock pickers versus indexers—to see who were winning the battle for new investment dollars. Utpal Bhattacharya and Neil Galpin found that there was no tool currently available to measure such things. It's easy to track which stocks are bought and sold in a given day, but because most of the transactions are anonymous, there's no way to say for sure whether those stocks are being bought by index funds allocating new investor dollars according to the index, or by actively managed funds putting new money into their latest stock picks, or by individual investors picking their own stocks. So Bhattacharya and Galpin created a measure.

Index funds, the two noted, mostly hold stocks in proportion to their market values. That is, they put more money into big companies and less money into small ones. If all investors were indexers, the dollar value of each stock's daily trading would be proportional to the company's size—big companies would have big dollar amounts of their shares traded each day. The difference between a stock's expected dollar volume and its actual one, the two reasoned, is due largely to stock picking.

Bhattacharya and Galpin put their measure to work on more than four decades of trading data and published the results in a 2005 paper titled "Is Stock Picking Declining Around the World?" Stock picking accounted for 60 percent of U.S. market volumes in the 1960s, but by the early 2000s that figure had fallen to 24 percent, the study found. Stock picking is more popular in emerging markets (that is, in the stock markets of recently poor countries that are now becoming less poor, like China), but it's on the decline everywhere.

That raises the question: Why should you do something that fewer investors are doing every day?

In what follows, I'll run through the history of how so many people came to believe the stock market can't be beat. I'll also explain why those people are wrong.

Why Stock Picking Isn't Supposed to Work

This is a story about ancient ovulation, a game of dice, twitchy molecules, and a stock-pricing machine that broke. It's the story of why, despite early, award-winning research to the contrary, you absolutely can beat the stock market. Above all, it's a story about math, some of its uses, and some of its limits.

Math isn't a science. It's a language. It's used to communicate ideas that are complex enough or repetitive enough to make describing them with words awkward. The simplest form of math is counting. You can say you bought an orange, an orange, an orange, an orange, and an orange. Or you can say you bought five oranges. There's nothing intuitive about *five*. It had to be created. And long before the word or number was created someone had to figure out that five apples, five rocks, and five marks in a tree all have something in common.

The earliest evidence of counting—the world's earliest math artifact—is the Lebombo bone. It's a piece of a baboon's calf bone with 29 notches found three decades ago in the mountains between South Africa and Swaziland. The notches aren't scrapes. They're clearly and intentionally carved. Someone was counting. Why 29? Two things operate in units of about 29: lunar cycles, on which early calendars were based, and menstrual cycles. (The words for month, menstrual, moon, and measure in Latin and Greek are closely related.) The world's first mathematician, it seems, might have been an ovulating African.

The math that led people to conclude stock picking is futile dates back to 1654 and the middle of the *Age of Reason*, when smart people the world over were using math and logic to demystify the world around them. A French writer with an interest in gambling named Antoine Gombaud, Chevalier de Méré (that's all one person) posed a question to a math-minded friend named Blaise Pascal. It concerned a popular game of the time in which two dice were thrown 24 times. De Méré wanted to know whether he should bet on the occurrence of at least one double-six during the 24 throws.

Pascal and a lawyer friend named Pierre de Fermat, who also had a head for numbers, mulled the problem over in a series of letters. Earlier mathematicians had solved isolated problems concerning games of chance. Pascal and Fermat came up with a general theory on calculating all such problems. A Dutch scientist named Christian Huygens published a book based on the letters a few years later. It was part math textbook, part gambling manual, and it detailed for the first time the theory of probability.

Probability theory is used to predict the outcome of random events. It can't tell you for sure whether you'll roll double sixes on a particular toss of a pair of dice. But it can tell you the likelihood of rolling double sixes on that toss. Over a large number of tosses, that likelihood tends to be reflected in the results. Probability theory was and is a big deal, and not just because of those Blackjack cheat sheets they hand out in casinos. Before the Age of Reason, people were more likely to turn to a soothsayer than a mathematician for odds making. Pascal and Fermat helped show that the language of math can be used to create rules gamblers can use to make money.

That got people thinking about how else to use probability to make sense of other random or seemingly random events. For example, in 1662, a London cloth merchant named John Graunt determined that you can predict when people will die, so long as you do it for a large group of people at the same time. Edmund Halley, who would have a comet named after him in 1682 by determining that it was the same one that passed by 75 years earlier and 76 years before that, found a group of people suitable for death-predicting in the town of Breslau, now part of Poland. The town had an archive containing detailed medical records of its residents, including age of death. Halley showed how the combination of Pascal's gambling math and Breslau's records could be used to profitably price "bets" for people to place on how long they'll live. Today that's called life insurance.

Probability seemed to be able to predict everything. It was only a matter of time before it was applied to stocks.

Molecules and Markets

Mathematical finance was born on March 29, 1900, albeit quietly. On that date a French student named Louis Bachelier won approval from University of Paris professors for defense of his doctoral thesis. Bachelier had studied physics and math. He had a particular interest in the theory of heat, now part of a larger field called *thermodynamics*, which ascribes things like temperature changes to motion and energy. (Previously, heat was thought to be an object—a weightless gas or fluid that naturally flows from warm bodies to cool ones.) For his thesis, though, Bachelier chose an oddball subject: investments, perhaps because of his experience at the Paris Stock Exchange, where he is believed to have worked. He called his paper "Theory of Speculation." It was an effort to take probability math derived from movements in the physical world and apply it to movements of investment prices.

Bachelier started with the assumption that the expected gain of one who speculates in investments at any given moment is zero. His paper looks at price changes during the years 1894 to 1898 in a popular investment of the day called *rente*, which was a perpetual government bond (that is, one that never matured) with a fixed interest rate. "Past, present and even discounted future events are reflected in market price, but often show no apparent relation to price changes," reads the first paragraph in Bachelier's paper. And further on: "If the market, in effect, does not predict its fluctuations, it does assess them as being more or less likely, and this likelihood can be evaluated mathematically."

To describe the movements of investments, Bachelier made a mathematical breakthrough in something called *Brownian motion*. It's named after Robert Brown, a Scottish botanist who noticed in 1827 that grains of pollen suspended in water could be seen oscillating when viewed under a microscope. (The mathematics of Brownian motion would be solved independently by Albert Einstein five years later and used to measure molecules.) Brownian motion is what's known as a *stochastic*, which is any process that is governed by laws of probability (like dice rolling).

Bachelier used Brownian motion to explain investment movements as what's now called a *martingale*. That's a stochastic (or probability process) for which the expected future value, considering past and present values, is equal to the present value. For example, if you flip a coin 100 times in a row and win $5 for each time it comes up heads while losing $5 each time it comes up tails, we would expect you to end up with the same amount of money you started with.

Bachelier's work anticipated later conclusions on the randomness of stock movements and the futility of trying to pick good stocks by half a century.

Upon reviewing Bachelier's paper, his professor seemed to understand that there were limits as to how far the findings could be stretched to predict real-world movements in investment prices: Here's a translation of the beginning of the professor's report. It's taken from a 2001 interview with University of Paris math professor Bernard Bru published in *Finance and Stochastics*.

> The subject chosen by Mr. Bachelier is somewhat removed from those which are normally dealt with by our applicants. His thesis is entitled "Theory of Speculation" and focuses on the application of probability to the stock market. First, one may fear that the author had exaggerated the applicability of probability as is often done. Fortunately, this is not the case. In his introduction and further in the paragraph entitled "Probability in Stock Exchange Operations," he strives to set limits within which one can legitimately apply this type of reasoning. He does not exaggerate the range of his results, and I do not think that he is deceived by his formulas.

Lousy Stock Pickers

Bachelier's work wouldn't take hold in the United States until it was rediscovered more than 60 years later. Other leading academics in the United States compared stock movements to random events in the 1920s and 1930s. One found them similar to the chance curve obtained by throwing dice. Another said they resembled lottery numbers.

America's stock-market meltdown in 1929, and the economic depression that followed, got investors wondering why no one had seen it coming. A Colorado businessman named Alfred Cowles set about studying whether professionals giving advice on which stocks to buy displayed any ability to beat the market. He found that they didn't. He showed that 16 financial firms making recommendations between 1928 and 1932 had lagged the average stock by 1.4 percent a year. He found that recommendations made by *Wall Street Journal* editor William D. Hamilton between 1904 and 1929 had also underperformed. He also found that picks made by 24 financial publications showed what he would later call "no evidence of skill." Later he extended that study by several years and found four times as many bullish recommendations as bearish ones, despite the fact that the stock market had performed awfully. The pickers showed no signs of good picking.

Things wouldn't get much better for stock pickers in later studies. In 1951 a Princeton University senior named John Bogle (remember that name) wrote a thesis paper titled "Mutual Funds Can Make No Claims of Superiority over the Market Averages." His research was backed up by numerous studies over the next two decades. A 1966 study in *Harvard Business Review* titled "Can Mutual Funds Outguess the Market," concluded that no, they can't. A 1968 study co-authored by Princeton economics professor Burton Malkiel (remember that name, too) found that not only can't Wall Street pros pick stocks, they can't forecast company profits, either. Even today, buy recommendations by Wall Street analysts don't generally do better than other stocks, and four out of five mutual fund managers underperform the broad market—but more on that later.

The Perfect Portfolio

Cowles founded and funded the Econometric Society in 1930 and the Cowles Commission for Economic Research in 1932. Both were created to study the application of mathematics to finance in order to gain insight into making business decisions and investing money. Harry Markowitz, a member of the Cowles Commission while a student at the University of Chicago, came up with a new way to build stock portfolios in 1952.

Investors until that time had made decisions on which stocks to buy by reviewing information about the companies. They looked at things like earnings, dividends, debt, and competition. Markowitz theorized in a series of papers starting with "Portfolio Theory," published in the *Journal of Finance* in 1952, that the most important information in determining whether you should buy a stock or any asset isn't contained in these *fundamental* attributes, but rather, in three statistical ones: average return, volatility of returns, and correlation with other assets.

Average return is simply the return that class of assets has generated in the past. *Volatility* is measured using standard deviation. In this context, it tries to predict how far away from the average return a single year's return is likely to be. It does so by measuring how far returns have strayed from the average in the past, and assuming the patterns will continue. It's closely related to something mentioned in the last chapter, that the risk of losing money in the stock market diminishes as you hold stocks longer. In any given year, stock returns can deviate far from the average, but over time, these deviations cancel each other out. Volatility, independent of any other piece of information, is an undesirable stock attribute. (Of course, whether you should try to reduce volatility depends on whether you can accurately forecast it using past volatility.)

Correlation is the relationship between two changing pieces of information, or variables. All variables are correlated, but some have strong positive correlations (they tend to move together), some have weak ones (they don't seem to relate to each other), and still others have negative ones (one tends to zig when the other zags). Note that correlation applies only to variables such as stock prices and not fixed information such as a guaranteed rate of return.

Markowitz theorized that stock returns and volatility are inseparable: Higher returns can't be achieved without taking on more volatility. He also determined that by combining different volatile investments, an investor could reduce the overall volatility of a portfolio, as long as these investments aren't perfectly correlated. A good year in one stock would offset a bad year in another, and so on. According to Markowitz, it does no good to seek stock returns without considering volatility. All investors want to reduce their portfolio volatility, and the way to do that is to combine stocks with differing correlations. The more of them you combine, the lower your portfolio volatility falls.

Markowitz is sometimes credited with discovering that risk and returns are related. That's not quite true. Financial practitioners before Markowitz's time had a general sense of risk. They knew that a widow of modest means should likely buy different stocks than a trust fund kid with a horse-racing form tucked under one arm. Further, Markowitz didn't incorporate risk, per se, into his study. He incorporated past volatility. It's sometimes confused with risk, but the two aren't nearly the same, as we'll see later.

Note, too, that stocks are generally regarded as having at least two types of risk: market risk and stock-specific risk. Market risk is the risk that your returns will be affected by external events such as wars, interest rate changes, and recessions. These can't be diversified away. Stock-specific risk is the risk that an individual stock will underperform the market. This risk can be diversified by combining different stocks. Whether the best way to do that involves looking at past volatility is debatable.

The Stock Pricer

Markowitz would later share a Nobel Prize in economics with William Sharpe. Sharpe took the math that Markowitz and others had developed, ran it through a frighteningly complex set of manipulations, and came up with a simple formula for investors to use to price stocks. Actually, the formula tells investors the return they should expect from a particular stock, but if you know how much you'll make on a stock, you can figure out how much you should pay for it. The formula looks something like this:

Expected return = Risk free rate + Beta * Risk premium

Expected return is what you're trying to determine, a return you can expect a particular stock to provide, for example. The risk-free rate is the rate available on a guaranteed investment. While academics can and do split hairs on the subject of what exactly constitutes *risk-free*, the more common rate to use for this purpose is the one paid on a U.S. government bond of short maturity, say 10 years. At the time of this writing, that was 4.5 percent. Beta is a measure of stock-specific risk. More on that in a

moment. Risk premium is the extra amount of return investors demand
to compensate for straying from the comfort of a risk-free investment.
If they can get 4.5 percent in a guaranteed investment, they're not
going to invest in stocks for the same return. Roughly speaking, if
stocks average a 10 percent yearly return before inflation, then investors,
who are determining prices through their buying and selling, want a
5.5 percent equity premium.

Figuring out the risk-free rate is easy. Determining the equity premium is more complicated than I've described it, but it is easy in concept,
at least. That leaves beta, or risk, as the only tricky part of the stock-
pricing formula. The formula is called the *Capital Asset Pricing Model*
(*CAPM*). Don't get caught pronouncing each letter, as in C-A-P-M.
All the cool people say *cap em*.

Risk is the only thing we need to figure out in order to have our
way with the stock market, it seems. If we know how risky a stock is,
we know what return to expect from it, which means we know how
much we should pay. So what is this magical measure? It's not all that
magical, really. Sharpe used past volatility to calculate it.

Past volatility is a poor substitute for risk. It says nothing about company information like financial strength to the extent that information
isn't reflected in past stock movements. Also, it looks at the past, which
isn't necessarily reflective of the future. For one thing, fast-growing companies would be expected to show far more trading volatility over the
past three years, when they were fighting to establish themselves, than
over the next three, when they'll enjoy more predictable profits.

The CAPM, like the work of Harry Markowitz, says that you can't
pick better stocks to achieve bigger returns. You can only pick "riskier"
ones. Since no one wants more risk, the model suggests that we shouldn't
try to pick great stocks. We should just buy as many stocks as we can
and let their various levels of risk offset each other.

Efficient Markets

The definitive paper on why stock picking is pointless is Eugene Fama's
1970 study "Efficient Capital Markets: A Review of Theory and Empirical Work." It put past findings on the subject together in what is

now called the *efficient markets hypothesis*. The hypothesis begins with a few basic assumptions. First, investors are rational in that they seek to maximize the value of their portfolios. Some investors might overreact to new information about stocks and others might underreact, but those reactions are random, and so they can't be predicted and exploited for profit. Second, people always want to make more money. Third, all investors have relatively free access to information and can buy and sell stocks easily. Given these assumptions and others, the hypothesis says that everything people know about a stock that could affect its price already has affected its price. In other words, a stock can't be a bargain based on the facts. If it was, people would have already bought it and pushed its price up, so that it wouldn't be a bargain anymore.

The efficient markets hypothesis is different from Bachelier's work on the randomness of stock movements, now called *random walk theory*, although the two are sometimes spoken of as if they are the same thing. The random walk theory says that a stock's past price movements can't be used to predict its future performance. The efficient markets hypothesis, or at least the strictest form of it, says that nothing can predict a stock's performance. That includes company financial statements, earnings forecasts, hands-on research, and so on. Trust the market to decide a stock's proper price, and don't try to outsmart the market, the hypothesis says.

Fama's work led to the creation of the following Wall Street joke about economists, which isn't that funny but is okay for a joke about economists: Two economists see a $100 bill lying on the street. One bends down to pick it up. The other stops him and says, "Why bother? If it was real someone would have already picked it up."

Chimps and Darts

The stock-picking-doesn't-work business was mostly confined to academics until the 1970s. Perhaps you've heard that a blindfolded chimpanzee throwing a dart at the stock quote pages of a newspaper has just a good a chance of landing on a winner as an expert money manager. Credit that imagery to Burton Malkiel, the Princeton professor I mentioned earlier who was unimpressed with the ability of Wall Street to forecast earnings. In his 1973 bestseller *A Random Walk Down Wall Street*, Malkiel addressed ordinary investors about why they shouldn't try to outsmart the market.

I've never quite understood why it has to be a chimp, by the way. Granted, chimps have short thumbs and that makes them terrible at darts. But surely a money manager losing to a blindfolded human in such a contest—even to a blindfolded money manager—would be humiliating enough to drive home the point: Stock picking is futile, and indexing is the only way to invest.

Remember John Bogle, that Princeton student and mutual fund critic? He turned the notion of efficient markets into a business. Since picking individual stocks does no good, and since investors are better off buying as many of them as they can, Bogle created a mutual fund that tracked the entire S&P 500 index. He launched it two years after Malkiel's book hit the shelves. It's the one I mentioned earlier that started with $11 million and now has more than 10,000 times that much—the Vanguard 500 fund. Money continues to pour into it.

We've come a long way from our ovulating African. The math has gotten complicated and the conclusions seem pretty grim for stock pickers. But things are about to get better.

Why Stock Picking Does Work

Warren Buffet and Peter Lynch are arguably the two best stock pickers of all time. If you had put $10,000 into Berkshire Hathaway, a struggling Massachusetts textile mill Buffet bought control of in 1965 and turned into a holding company for other investments, you'd have more than $78 million now. You'd have barely more than half a million if you had owned an index fund based on the S&P 500 over that time. We looked at Lynch's astounding returns earlier. Recall that he beat the S&P 500 by an average of 13 percentage points a year during the 13 years he managed the Magellan mutual fund for Fidelity investments.

Buffet and Lynch are obviously not fans of the efficient markets hypothesis. "I'd be a bum on the street with a tin cup if the markets were always efficient," Buffett is credited with saying. Lynch once quipped in a 1995 interview with *Fortune* magazine, "Efficient Markets? That's a bunch of junk, crazy stuff."

I'd love to cite the success of Buffet and Lynch as evidence that stock picking works. But I can't.

A few money managers will always make a killing in the stock market through luck, not skill. That's true even over long time periods. I'm not saying Buffett and Lynch aren't skilled. I'm saying I can't prove they are, mathematically. A single investor who picks stocks randomly has a 50 percent chance of beating the market. The chances of that investor beating the market ten years in a row is much smaller: about 0.1 percent. But there are thousands of money managers. The chances of one investor in a group of 1,000 producing a 10-year win streak is 63 percent. With 10,000 investors, it's a near certainty.

So the existence of good stock pickers doesn't prove stock picking works. The existence of clues that predict large stock returns, though, does. After all, stock prices are supposed to already reflect all available clues. If we find clues that consistently predict which stocks will perform well and which won't, the stock market must not be all that efficient. And there are plenty such clues.

The First Good Clues

A finance professor named Sanjoy Basu found a clue in 1977. He looked at share price histories for 1,400 companies between 1956 and 1971 and found something that seemed to predict far-better-than-average stock returns. It was the ratio of a stock's price to the earnings per share the company had generated over the past year: the price/earnings ratio (P/E). Basu didn't come up with the idea of the P/E. Stock pickers had long used it to gauge how expensive a stock is relative to the stream of profits that stock investors lay claim to. For example, Benjamin Graham, the man Warren Buffet credits with teaching him how to pick stocks, used the P/E extensively in books he wrote like "Securities Analysis," published in 1934, and "The Intelligent Investor," published in 1949. Of course, Basu had access to some things Graham didn't have, which allowed him to perform more thorough research on the P/E. First, he had the CAPM, the formula for determining how much stocks *should* return based on their past volatility. Second, he had magnetic tapes containing information on things like past stock prices and company earnings. Third, he had a computer to make sense of the recorded data.

Basu found that returns for low-P/E stocks during his study period exceeded those for high-P/E stocks by seven percentage points a year. He also found that the low P/E stocks didn't show higher levels of risk (volatility, really).

That was a problem. Recall that the CAPM says a stock's return is determined only by its risk as gauged by its volatility, and not by other factors, like its P/E. And the CAPM is part of the foundation of the efficient markets hypothesis, which says stock picking is futile.

Basu's results showed what are called *abnormal returns*. Economists use that term to describe returns that disagree with models created by, well, economists. (A little presumptuous, no? Who's to say the returns aren't normal and the models aren't abnormal?) Some people use terms like *excess risk-adjusted returns*. That means the same thing: that the returns exceed those predicted by models like the CAPM, which adjust for risk. Money managers call such returns *alpha*. I prefer to use something less medicinal and more celebratory like *fat returns* or *big gains*. That's admittedly less precise, but also less ugly.

A Swiss economist named Rolf Banz helped Basu break the CAPM. In 1981, he published a study in the *Journal of Financial Economics* titled "The Relationship Between Return and the Market Value of Common Stocks." It showed the returns to investing in small companies between 1931 and 1975. By small, I mean companies with low market values relative to other companies. A company's market value, recall, is what it would cost to buy all of its outstanding shares. Banz found that shares of the 50 smallest companies listed on the New York Stock Exchange outperformed those of the 50 largest companies by 1 percent a month on a risk-adjusted basis (volatility-adjusted, really). That's an enormous out-performance, akin to beating the stock market like Peter Lynch, only for 44 years instead of 13. This discovery was a problem, too. Just as the CAPM hadn't said anything about low-P/E stocks producing fat returns, it didn't say anything about small-company stocks producing them.

The New Stock Pricer

By now William Sharpe's CAPM was smoking and leaking radiator fluid. In 1992, Eugene Fama, who needed the CAPM to show that stock picking doesn't work, joined with another researcher, Kenneth French, to give it a tune-up.

Fama and French didn't dispute that P/Es and company size can be used to predict fat stock returns, phenomena now called the *value effect* and *size effect*. But also, they didn't concede that factors other than risk determine a stock's returns. That only leaves one choice. If the two clues predict fat returns, but only risk predicts fat returns, then the two clues must themselves be measures of risk.

Small companies, they reckoned, are riskier than big ones because they're not as stable. Also, low-P/E stocks are riskier than high-P/E ones. That might sound like the opposite of what you're used to hearing. If you buy stocks, you probably figure low-P/E ones are *less* risky than high-P/E ones because when you put up less money to capture a given amount of earnings, you're at risk of losing less. Fama and French saw things differently. To them, the fact that a stock's P/E is low means the share price must be lower than it should be, which means the stock is viewed by other investors as being flawed. The flaws those other investors see make the stock risky.

Beta, it seemed, was incomplete. Remember that beta is the risk measure that forms the most important part of the CAPM formula, and it is based on past volatility. Fama and French created a new beta by making adjustments for the size and value effect, their two new risk factors. Note that while they used market value to judge the size effect, they elected to use the price/book (P/B) ratio instead of the P/E to judge the value effect. The P/B ratio shows a company's share price relative to its book value per share. Book value is essentially the amount of money a company would get if it liquidated its assets. Fame and French chose P/B for their model because they found it to eclipse P/E in terms of its ability to predict big stock gains.

This new stock pricer is called the *Fama/French three-factor model*. It doesn't have a cool nickname like cap em. I doubt that, say, *FaFre Three-FaMo* will catch on.

The three-factor model is the current standard for disputing the ability of investors to beat the stock market. A clue might be able to beat the volatility-adjusted returns predicted by the CAPM, but believers of the efficient markets hypothesis hold that it surely won't be able to beat the volatility-, size- and value-adjusted returns predicted by the three-factor model.

More Good Clues

In fact, many clues do beat the three-factor model. For example, the clues that form the basis for the stock screening strategies in this book all beat it. Let's look at two examples.

When companies report that their profits for a given quarter have surpassed those that Wall Street had forecast, shares of those companies tend to produce great returns long after the reports are out. Researchers call that *post-earnings announcement drift*, or PEAD. Studies as far back as the 1960s and as recently as 2006 show that PEAD-based strategies work and work well, beating the market by several percentage points a year. The "Surprise, Surprise" strategy detailed in Chapter 14 takes this a step further by looking for earnings surprises that are accompanied by sales surprises. (More on these terms later.) It has been shown to beat the market by twice as much as a typical PEAD-based strategy, even after adjusting for "risk" using the three-factor model.

Stocks with strong price performance over the past six months to a year also tend to beat the market, but only for another six months to a year, on average. That's called the *momentum effect*, and researchers have known about it for more than a decade. In Chapter 12 we'll look at a better way to gauge share price momentum that has been shown to produce enormous returns, even after adjusting for the three-factor model. The returns tend to last for much longer than six months to a year.

There are many other clues that predict great stock returns. The amount of money companies spend on research can be used to tell you where their stocks are likely headed (see Chapter 15). So can the amount of money bosses spend to buy shares of their own companies (Chapter 19). This book doesn't cover strategies based on all the clues, but it does cover strategies based on the best clues I've found. That is, it covers strategies based on the best clues other people have found, which I have stolen.

Stock Picking Survives

It's not that those brainy stock-pricing models like the CAPM and the three-factor model are wrong. It's that, to the extent those models are wrongly applied to things like finding great stocks, they're incomplete. They're also a bit incestuous, mathematically speaking.

To the extent that clues beat the models, the models are incomplete. When we find a good clue, we can continue fine-tuning the models by calling that clue a new risk factor. For example, we can say that somehow companies whose bosses are buying shares are riskier than other companies, because their returns are higher, and because the models hold that higher returns must be due to risk. But all we'd be doing is continuously turning the thing we're looking for (fat returns) into the thing we're using to find it (risk) in order to say that the thing we're looking for doesn't exist.

Investors can use what's now called *modern portfolio theory*, the set of findings on things like diversification and risk-adjusted returns, to improve real-world portfolio results, but only by applying them broadly. For example, it makes sense to reduce the overall risk of a stock portfolio by choosing great stocks that tend to move in different ways. We'll look shortly at the difference between *growth* and *value* stocks, which tend to complement each other nicely. But blindly applying past-volatility math to stocks, or applying a size or value calculation to them, calling the result *risk*, and saying it determines returns isn't the way to go about finding great stocks.

At the beginning of this chapter we saw how the language of math can be applied to real-world problems in order to make accurate predictions. Over the past 100 years, market researchers seem to have put math to work beyond its role as a language, using it instead as a source of knowledge about things that, at least for now, are too complex for the language of math to fully tackle. The next chapter is virtually math-free. In it, we'll see some of the things that math models aren't quite up to predicting yet.

It's possible to beat the stock market. In fact, now might be a better time than ever to do so.

With all that money flowing into index funds, fewer people are trying to pick stocks. Recall that Bhattacharya and Galpin showed that stock picking as a percentage of overall trading has declined from 60 percent in the 1960s to about 24 percent as of a couple of years ago. As more people give in to indexing and fewer people try to pick underpriced stocks, there are fewer people available to make those ongoing price adjustments on which the efficient markets hypothesis depends. In other words, if no one trades on new information because everyone thinks it's already priced in, the new information doesn't get priced in. That's a restatement of something called *the Gossman and Stiglitz paradox*. Bhattacharya and Galpin used that paradox to predict just how unpopular stock picking will become, since it can't, by definition, disappear. They put the figure at 11 percent.

Stock picking, already less than half as popular as it was in the 1960s, will likely be less than half as popular as it is today sometime in the future. That means fewer people will be competing against you to find great stocks.

This book is about stock-picking strategies that beat the broad market's returns. When someone tells me about a market-beating strategy, I usually ask one question right away. I like to ask it in a down-home but vaguely accusatory voice, like Jed Clampett questioning the bank manager, but maybe I've just watched too many episodes of *The Beverly Hillbillies*. The question is . . .

Chapter 3

If Stock Picking Strategies Work, Why Haven't They Been Used Up?

In the last chapter I mentioned a stock-picking strategy based on earnings surprises. I noted that it has sharply outperformed the broad stock market for more than 40 years after its discovery. How can that be? Earnings surprises are one of the easiest things for investors to track. Earnings data are listed on most financial Web sites and surprises are often covered in the daily news. If investors know stocks are likely to go up for a long time after companies beat earnings estimates, why wouldn't they buy those stocks right away, thereby pushing their prices up, and thereby rendering the strategy dead?

The answer to that question reveals a key flaw in the *efficient markets hypotheses*, which says that stock picking is futile. The hypothesis is based on a number of assumptions about markets and behavior. For stock picking to be possible, one or more of those assumptions must be wrong.

The hypothesis assumes that people can buy and sell stocks cheaply and easily. A stock trade today costs $10 and often less and can be made in a matter of seconds, so that seems like a fair assumption. The hypothesis assumes people have equal access to information. I think that's fair to say, too. It's illegal to trade on information that hasn't been made available to the public. Professional money managers might turn readily available information into new, exotic forms—stock-pricing models and such—that the rest of us can't figure out, and we could call that a barrier to information. But the record of such money managers suggests their information isn't that valuable. Mutual funds, on average, underperform the broad stock market, remember. Also, the market-beating clues we've looked at so far aren't fancy. Each one took only a few sentences to explain.

That leaves the behavioral assumptions. The efficient markets hypothesis assumes people always act in a way that maximizes their wealth. Also, it assumes people, on average, respond rationally to new information. Turns out, they don't.

The study of why investors don't always act the way they should is called *behavioral finance*. It combines economics and finance with psychology, and it's a fairly new field of study. Just as econometrics uses math to try to figure out where we should put our money, behavioral finance uses psychology to figure out why we don't always put our money where we should. People sometimes act irrationally, or at least, in ways that seem irrational. Those actions produce mispriced stocks—stocks that are cheaper or more expensive than stock-pricing models or even company fundamentals suggest they should be. Informed investors can use that information to find stock bargains.

Nutty Behavior

Let's look at some odd financial decisions people sometimes make. Then we'll look at why they might make them.

Anchoring

Go to a mattress store to see anchoring in action. Retail mattress sales are one of the shadiest businesses in America. Mattress makers use different model names, depending on the store they sell through. One company's "Ambassador" for sale at Sleepy's may or may not be similar to their "Diplomat" at 1–800-Mattress—it's anyone's guess. That's to keep customers from seeking better prices. I can't imagine the Federal Trade Commission will allow the practice to continue for another decade. But this isn't *Consumer Reports*; my interest in mattress stores is that the blind haggling they produce makes them great for seeing behavioral finance in action.

Ever notice how the salesperson starts with a wildly high price and sometimes comes down by $1,000 or more? He knows about anchoring. He might not know the name for it, but experience has taught him that if he starts with a shockingly high price and then moves down to a politely high one, you might view the politely high price as a comparative bargain.

Investors use anchoring when they buy a stock that has plunged 50 percent without having a good reason to do so. They're anchored in the price it was trading at before the plunge. That makes the new one look like a bargain.

Post-earnings announcement drift, or the tendency of stocks to move higher after positive earnings surprises, might be caused in part by anchoring. Analysts are slow to increase their remaining earnings estimates to reflect the full measure of good news contained in positive earnings surprises, studies show. They seem anchored in their old estimates. As they gradually come around and increase their estimates, stock prices drift higher.

Representativeness

My friend Sarah is 28, likes yoga, and has a piercing in one of her eyebrows. Based on that description, which of the following statements would you guess to be true about Sarah?

1. She eats meat and vegetables.
2. She's a vegetarian.
3. She's a vegetarian and has a tattoo.

I made Sarah up, so I can't give you the answer. But if you guessed anything but the first choice, you went against the odds. Just 3 percent of Americans are vegetarians. And while I don't know the exact odds of a 28-year-old female having a tattoo, and while they're surely not low enough, they're plenty low. The odds are even lower that someone would be vegetarian *and* have the tattoo.

Maybe you guessed the second choice because you know people who are into yoga and who also don't eat meat. Or maybe you guessed the worst choice, the last choice, because you know people who have piercings and tattoos. If so, you chose based on something called *representativeness*. That's the tendency to evaluate an uncertain event based on how similar it is to events you've observed in the past.

Investors use representativeness when, for example, they fail to recognize real signs of improvement in companies that have disappointed them in the past. They've already labeled those companies as losers, because that has been their experience. Now they can't see that those stocks are bargains, even when the facts suggest they are.

Gambler's Fallacy

If you regularly play your kids' birthdays as lottery numbers, or if you always sit at the same slot machine when you go to a casino, you might be using the *gambler's fallacy*. That's the belief that random events are likely to happen because of a series of past events. For example, there's no reason to stick with a slot machine just because you feel it's due, just as there's no reason to believe that a coin flip that comes up heads 10 times in a row will come up tails the next time.

Investors succumb to the gambler's fallacy when they sell a stock merely because it keeps going up every day. They do the same thing when they hold a falling stock, figuring it just has to come back.

Herd Behavior

People will do some remarkable things simply because everyone else is doing them. They'll speed, yawn, kill, jump nude into icy water, grow mullets, and pretend to like cigars (usually not all at once).

Herd behavior is easy to see in the stock market. Crashes and bubbles happen when investors follow each other and not the facts.

Overconfidence

Three-quarters of mutual fund managers surveyed for a 2006 study rated their performance as better than average. Almost all of the rest said they were average. That clearly can't be true. Half must be below average. That's the definition of average (or at least, it's the definition of something called median, which is close enough).

Studies show that overconfident investors (most of them) trade too often and produce poor returns.

Risk Aversion

Suppose you own two stocks: Painful Industries and Hold On To Your Hat Technologies. Painful has gone straight down since you bought it. Hold On has soared.

What should you do? There's a case to be made for holding on to Hold On, based on the price momentum effect. But let's say you don't know about that. In that case, you should do the same thing you always do: Size up each stock based on its current prospects and not its past performance. Typically investors don't do either. Overwhelmingly, they sell the winner and keep the loser.

They do so because they feel the pain of losses more acutely than the pleasure of gains. If you've ever sulked for a week after a losing investment but moved right on after a winning one, you know what that's like. Risk aversion causes investors to act based on embedded gains and losses rather than likely returns.

Why We Do Strange Things

The aforementioned examples of nutty behavior have something in common. They defy the mathematics of probability. Traditional economics holds that people always make financial choices in such a way as to maximize their wealth, or their probability of achieving wealth. That makes it pretty easy to calculate which choices people will make. The set of mathematics used to do that is called *utility theory*. It uses probability to determine how people should spend their resources in order to get the most satisfaction. But sometimes people make choices that go against probability. Is it that people don't always want more money, or that they just have trouble figuring things out? Behavioral finance holds that it's a little bit of both.

We're Not Always Greedy

Examples of non–wealth-maximizing behavior are all around us. Suppose you're out of town. I mean, *way* out of town. I'm talking *Children of the Corn,* here. You've never seen this place before. You're never coming back. But you're hungry. You pull into the only diner in town and order a hamburger.

The burger's good. You have no complaints about the service, either. And the check says it's only $8—nice. You lay a ten on the table, and you're out the door.

How dare you. You just left a tip at a restaurant that you're never going to visit again. That means you're out the $2, and there's no chance you'll be compensated for it with more good service in the future. That's not very wealth-maximizing of you. How can we expect the stock market to be efficient when you're throwing money around all willy-nilly?

Perhaps you invest in a socially responsible mutual fund. You don't want your money going into companies that make bad products or do mean things. For example, you don't care for cigarette makers because of that pesky they-kill-their-customers factor. So you don't want to buy their stocks no matter how cheap they seem. That's not wealth-maximizing. Maybe it is if you believe that moral behavior carries an economic benefit, such as fewer lawsuits or more customer loyalty. But these are called *socially* responsible funds, not *economically* responsible funds. That tells me they're trying to be good even if it means giving up a couple of bucks.

Have you heard of *dollar cost averaging*? That's the tactic of investing your money in a mutual fund little by little in regular dollar amounts each quarter. Financial advisors recommend it all the time as a way to reduce risk and maximize returns. I've got news for you. They're wrong. If you have a big chunk of money to invest, you're statistically better off investing it all at once rather than little by little. That's because the market at any one point is more likely to go up than down, and if you're fully invested you're more likely to capture those gains. But people dollar cost average anyway even though it doesn't maximize their wealth, and for good reason—doing so makes them more comfortable.

In the 1970s and early 1980s, a pair of psychologists named Daniel Kahneman and Amos Tversky conducted a series of experiments dealing with choices and risk. They learned some strange things about how people make decisions that aren't nearly predicted by utility theory.

Consider what economists now call the *Asian disease problem.* I've never quite understood why the disease has to be Asian, but then, I was confused by the chimps and darts thing, too.

The United States is preparing for the outbreak of a rare Asian disease. Scientists predict 600 people will die. But there's hope. Two plans to combat the disease have been proposed. Scientists have calculated the odds of each plan succeeding. It's up to you to decide which plan to follow.

> Program A: If Program A is adopted, 200 people will be saved.
> Program B: If program B is adopted, there's a one-third probability that all 600 will be saved and a two-thirds probability that no one will be saved.

Which will it be?

If you have a head for these things you know your choice doesn't matter. Programs A and B are statistical equals. But, you say, how can I be so cold? These are real lives we're talking about. These people are going to die. Surely saving 200 people for certain is better than rolling the dice.

You're not nearly alone if you feel that way. Nearly three-quarters of respondents in the experiment picked Program A.

Then things got nuttier. A second group of subjects were told of the same disease. They were given the same two choices, only the choices were presented as follows.

> Program C: If Program C is adopted, 400 people will die.
> Program D: If Program D is adopted, there's a one-third probability that no one will die and a two-thirds probability that 600 people will die.

Again, it's a statistical toss-up between the programs. But taking a shot at saving people sounds better than taking no shot. More than three-quarters of respondents picked the second program this time.

This experiment and similar ones led Kahneman and Tversky to some conclusions about behavior that didn't show up in the straight probability math of utility theory. People place a higher value on a certain gain than a merely probable gain, even when the two are statistically equal. They do just the opposite when it comes to losses. People lock in gains quickly because a sure gain at today's price is better than an unsure one at a higher price. And they hold losers forever because, well, screw it, it feels better to have a shot at a gain than to have a sure loss. Such non–wealth-maximizing behavior leads investors to make chronically bad decisions about which of their stocks to replace and when.

Kahneman and Tversky shaped their findings into a new utility theory that better accounts for the way people feel about gains and losses. It's called *prospect theory*. Out of it flows not only the notion of loss aversion, but also something called *framing*, which is the tendency of people to change their choices depending on how the choices are presented, just like they did in the Still-Not-Sure-Why-It's-Asian-Disease Problem.

Non–wealth-maximizing behavior could be responsible for some of the market inefficiencies we've seen—the clues that tend to produce fat gains. But I don't know how big of an impact it has. The efficient markets hypothesis doesn't say that every last person has to act in a way that maximizes wealth. It just says that a large number of people must do so, enough to ensure those market-beating clues get gobbled up. Surely some people can overcome their wealth-wasting tendencies with logic and make statistically accurate choices.

More compelling would be an explanation that doesn't depend on how we feel about the choices, but how we see them to begin with. If a tendency to make odd decisions is hard-wired into us as humans, after all, there's not much that logic can do about it.

Sometimes We Don't See So Well

Have a look at Figure 3.1. Which of the two vertical line segments looks longer to you? Put that tape measure down. Eyes only.

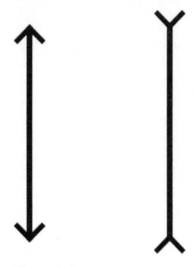

Figure 3.1

I'm guessing you said they're equal length. But I'm guessing you only said that because you've seen it before. That's cheating. You're supposed to say the one on the right looks longer, because it does.

The drawing is a well-known example of optical illusions. Vision is complicated. The amount of information your eyes take in from moment to moment is absurdly large. People act like high-definition television is such a big deal. "I only had 480 lines of resolution on my old set," they say. "Then I went to 720. Now I have 1,080. This picture looks amazing." You want *really* high definition? Look out a window. I swear, there must be a skajillion lines of resolution out there.

Processing all that information before making decisions would be impossible, especially when those decisions have to be made on the fly. Imagine a stray softball is heading for your privates.

Let me back up. Imagine you're a man, even if you're not. Now imagine a stray softball is heading for your privates. I took an entire class in school that deals with telling for sure whether said softball is, in fact, going to collide with said privates. It's called physics. I don't remember all of it, but there were speeds and trajectories involved, and gravity was in there somewhere. If your calculus is good and if you can accurately gauge the inputs, you'll know for certain where that softball is headed and what you should do. But you'll have sore privates well before you finish the math.

Because the information is so complex and the stakes are so high, people have evolved with the ability to take mental shortcuts in making decisions. These shortcuts are called *heuristics*, and they're important. Rather than break out their scientific calculators, people judge the path of that softball by fixing their gaze on it and judging how the angle of their gaze changes. Early humans that hadn't evolved these heuristics were at a serious disadvantage to ones that had. They wouldn't have been able to quickly judge, say, whether an approaching enemy was likely to catch them. So they were more likely to die before reproducing. Also, they were terrible at softball.

Perfectly useful heuristics can cause people to make mental mistakes when they're misapplied, though. The right line in the optical illusion looks longer than the left one because you're using a mental shortcut in a situation where you don't need one. The tails on those lines are designed to make them appear three-dimensional. The inverted arrow heads on the right line make it look farther away than the left one. You've evolved in such a way as to see a far-away object as larger than it appears at first, just as it is in a three-dimensional world, on the off chance that the far-away object wants to catch and eat you. That kept your ancestors from mistaking lions for ants, perhaps. But that heuristic doesn't work well when you look at lines on a page that is, for practical purposes, two-dimensional. It tells you that the line that's made to appear farther away is longer when it's really not.

Investors use heuristics often, even when they don't mean to. Researchers Richard Thaler and Werner DeBondt explored that subject in a 1994 paper titled "Financial Decision-Making in Markets and Firms: A Behavioral Perspective." Several of the nutty behaviors covered earlier flowed from that work. If these behaviors are hard-wired into our brains, we're not being nutty at all. We're just using the tools we have to make decisions. Some of those tools, like representativeness, might leave beaten-down stocks too cheap because we fail to acknowledge them as bargains. Others, like anchoring, might leave fast-rising stocks too cheap because we're still mentally attached to the low price, and can't get used to paying the high one.

Again, behavioral finance is fairly new. Not all economists are thrilled with it. Some feel that because it doesn't lend itself to mathematical proofs, it's not a real science. In fact, it's not a science. But then, economics isn't a science, either.

If you're not predicting the motion of physical objects, you're not using science. Physics and chemistry are sciences. They predict the motion of cannonballs and molecules, respectively. Economics, like the psychology that drives behavioral finance, is a social study. It's called *social* because it involves human behavior.

Applying the language of math to the study of human behavior, as econometrics does, doesn't result in science. Universities sometimes make it sound as though it does. They call economics a social "science" in their course catalogs. But they only give it that name to differentiate it from their actual science courses. Otherwise they'd just label economics and physics *science*.

The CAPM and the three-factor model we looked at in the last chapter don't fully predict stock prices, because stock prices are driven in part by human behavior. To come up with a true stock-pricing model you'd have to be able to predict human behavior. To do that, you'd have to be able to fully model human behavior in the physical world, so that you can use science to describe it. That is, you'd have to understand every last hormone swoosh and brain cell spark as clearly as we understand the movement of billiard balls. For now, science recognizes an inevitable amount of uncertainty when it comes to physical motion on the most finite level. (Otherwise, we'd eventually be able to fully model the physical world, including the part of it responsible for human behavior, which would allow us to effectively see the future and know the past—but I'm not trying to write a science fiction novel here.)

Don't expect to have a fully efficient stock market anytime soon. To make sense of stocks you'll have to rely on not-quite-sciences like psychology mixed with economics, or behavioral finance. The good news is that the uncertainty involved leaves plenty of stock bargains out there for you to find.

Our early human ancestors left us with a great set of tools for hunting: We follow others, guess outcomes based on past experience, panic, and sometimes run. But our ancestors were lousy stock pickers. The brains they left us aren't equipped for locating great stocks in a sea of ordinary ones. What we need to find those stocks is a tool.

Chapter 4

Stock Screening Is the Best Way to Find Great Stocks

S tock screening is neither exotic nor new. Stripped to its core, it's simply the process of choosing among stocks using facts rather than hunches. If you're familiar with stock screening, you know that your computer plays a big role. But the computer just allows you to evaluate more stocks and more facts at the same time than you would be able to evaluate with a pencil and paper. Your success depends more on how good of a strategy you use—which clues you look for—than it does on the computer you have and which stock-screening tool you decide to use.

Smart investors, after all, have screened potential stock investments since before the creation of the World Wide Web (1989), the personal computer (1975), or even the early, outdoor predecessor to the New

York Stock Exchange (1792). They've screened ever since they had more than one stock to choose from.

400-Year-Old Technology

They've had such a choice, believe it or not, for nearly four centuries. An investor in Amsterdam in 1625 might have been faced with the decision of whether to buy shares of the Dutch East India Company or the Dutch West India Company. Neither would have made its way into one of today's socially responsible mutual funds. The first was incorporated through a merger of smaller sea merchants in 1602, and granted a monopoly by the States-General of the Netherlands for colonizing, trading with, and otherwise exploiting Asia. The second, chartered in 1620, was given a trade monopoly in the Caribbean and jurisdiction over the slave routes between West Africa, Brazil, the Caribbean, and North America.

Dutch East is generally considered the world's first stock. If you saw the 2004 heist film *Ocean's Twelve*, you might remember the thieves going to Amsterdam to steal the world's oldest stock certificate. It read "V.O.C." at the top, which stands for *Vereenigde Oostindische Compagnie*. Translated to English, that means United East Indies Company. (There was no need to call it Dutch East until there was a British East, French East, and so on.) There were earlier stocks than Dutch East, really. If we extend the definition to include all companies that issue shares that represent a split of the profits, we can count sea-trading ventures from hundreds of years earlier.

The history of stocks is tied closely to the history of shipwrecks. There's something about floating one's wealth over open seas that inspires thoughts of sharing start-up capital and risk, even if it means sharing profits, too. However, most of those companies set out planning to fold after a single voyage to make sure profits were split fairly. Dutch East kept rolling, partly because of a profit-distributing innovation we'll look at in Chapter 16—dividends. Dutch East was also the first stock that could be easily bought and sold among investors. A stock exchange was created for that purpose, the world's first, in Amsterdam.

By 1625 Dutch East had produced a spotty but improving record of profits and dividends. Dutch West at that time was merely a start-up, but one with plenty of potential. An investor choosing between the two would have perhaps based his decision on some but not all of the clues available to you today, among them: dividend yields and payment histories, past profit growth, return on assets, trailing price/earnings ratios, and forecasts for next year's profits.

Dutch East turned out to be the better investment, if you're curious. It became the world's richest company and had a nearly two-century run, paying dividends that sometimes topped 60 percent a year. Dutch West folded in 1674, producing far skimpier returns before doing so.

New and Vastly Improved

Your task is, on the whole, easier than that of your seventeenth-century Dutch counterpart. That is, in one respect it has become more challenging, but in another it is far easier, and not just because today's company names are mostly easier to pronounce than *Vereenigde Oostindische Compagnie*.

More Challenging

The stock market isn't efficient, but it's far more efficient than it was. Information was difficult to come by in the days of Dutch East, and that meant that not everyone got their hands on the most useful facts. The enterprising investor gained an advantage over other investors through shear effort—looking over the company's assets, chatting with management, coming up with new ways to calculate the value of shares, and so on.

You're not likely to gain any informational advantages today. Companies are expressly forbidden to give useful information to a few investors without giving it to all of them. The strategies we'll look at, keep in mind, are based on other investors misreading or ignoring information, not on them not having access to it.

Also, there are far more stock investors today. That means that, even though stock picking is becoming rarer, there are more people competing against you to find great stocks.

Finally, there is a sea of information. Financial reports, analyst research, trading data, and more combine to create an overwhelming flow of numbers to sift through. Without a methodical approach to taming that information, an investor can easily become overwhelmed.

But Easier, Really

Computers and software make harnessing all that information easy. Cheap, online trading makes buying the stocks you want almost effortless. Although there are more investors competing for great stocks, there are far more stocks to choose from, too.

Chats with company managers and trips to the warehouse or shipyard won't yield as much useful information, but they are not time-efficient ways to search the entire stock market anyway. The goal of stock screening is to compare as many companies as possible to find the clues you want, and to focus your subsequent research on just those companies.

It's probably an unhealthy sign when someone starts comparing stock-screening to romance, but here goes.

It's Like Online Dating

That's right. If you've been with your current honeybunch for years, you probably met through one of the old-fashioned ways, like ignoring your company's don't-date-your-coworkers rule, or by going with a friend to places that combine big crowds with alcohol. But if you're single and looking, you'd be hurting your chances of finding the right person by not using one of those online personal ad services like Match.com.

Think about it. People go to singles bars because that's where the singles are. But there's no filtering mechanism. You can't proclaim what kind of mate you're looking for on the way in the door. Well, you can, but I don't think it will work. And using your worksite as a sober singles bar is fine, but you're restricting your choices to people you happen to bump into. How big of a field is that? What if you work at an Arctic research lab?

With online dating, you can screen for the attributes that are important to you before you even meet someone: nonsmoking, likes pets, works out, whatever. Not everyone that turns up on the search will be a perfect match, and you'll have to do some further research on your best candidates before knowing if things are going to work. But you choose from thousands of candidates instead of a few, and you focus your time on the ones most likely to be good matches.

Stock screening is like that, but with some important improvements. Long-distance relationships are not only okay, they're encouraged. Long-term relationships are ideal, but breakups are easy. The candidates are generally truthful about their profiles. And you can be far more specific; instead of assuming "likes to work out" means fit, you can screen for the equivalent of "falls within one standard deviation of the government guidelines for optimal body mass index" and "is generally considered attractive by a consensus of professional beauty judges." Whatever.

Stock screening is the best way to find great stocks. That's so because, whether you realize it or not, you are the best stock picker you know. I'm not just kissing up. Consider the alternatives.

The Alternatives Are Lousy

If you're not finding great stocks yourself using stock-screening software, you're probably hearing about stocks from someone else. You'll never have to go far to look for a stock recommendation. They cost nothing to make, and the people who make them have plenty to gain. Investment firms stand to gain fees if they can attract your business. Media outlets gain advertiser dollars if they can hold your attention. Even people you know gain a measure of respect by asserting their knowledge of the stock market. But following all these stock recommendations is probably a bad idea. Let's take a closer look at some of the people who want to advise you.

Mutual Fund Managers

Most actively managed mutual funds underperform the index funds they compete against. In a then-versus-now survey of the mutual fund industry published in 2005 in the *Financial Analysts Journal*, Vanguard founder John Bogle showed that actively managed stock funds lagged the S&P 500 index by an average of 1.7 percentage points a year during the 20 years ended 1965 and by 2.7 percentage points a year during the

20 years ended 2003. Let's look at some of the things that lead to that poor performance.

American mutual funds are among the most strictly regulated investment products in the world. Some of the restrictions are meant to keep investors safe, but often they merely keep them from achieving fat returns. Mutual funds are prohibited from placing more than 5 percent of their assets in any one stock. They don't hold 20 stocks; that would put them at the threshold. They hold far more stocks, often more than 100. Ask a couple of mutual fund managers which stocks they truly love and each might give you a list of eight. What about the other ones? Unlike a fund manager, you're free to buy just the eight stocks you love.

Mutual funds are also prohibited from owning more than 10 percent of the outstanding shares of another company. That makes it difficult for a $1 billion mutual fund to buy a meaningful stake in, say, a fast-growing chain of retail stores with a current market value of $100 million, no matter how much the fund manager likes the stock. It's easy for you, though.

Mutual fund managers also have to keep customers happy. At the end of each quarter, mutual funds must prepare reports for shareholders that show, among other things, the holdings of the fund. To make their presentations look better, some mutual funds sell their worst-performing stocks just before the quarter's end and replace them with high fliers. That's called *window dressing*. It doesn't help your returns. In fact, it hurts them if you consider the trading fees. You don't have to run your stock portfolio like a quarterly beauty contest.

Fund managers have to worry about falling too far behind those stock indexes they're supposed to beat. Many protect their jobs by simply buying into an index with a large portion of the money they're supposed to be picking stocks with. What are you paying those management fees for?

Speaking of fees, the mutual fund business may top even retail mattress stores when it comes to ugly pricing tactics. All mutual funds pay for their operating expenses and management fees by, naturally, deducting them from the fund. Some funds deduct more than five times as much money as others for similar services.

Many also impose a hefty sales charge that serves mostly to reimburse a salesperson for the work of talking you into buying the fund. These sales charges often range from 4 percent to 6 percent. (Some funds hide those fees in ways I could spend a chapter on. Suffice it to say that if a fund doesn't charge you up front but requires you to stay in for several years, someone probably got paid to sell you that fund, and their pay is probably being being taken out of your holdings.) Suppose I told you to go out and beat the stock market, but that you have to start out down 5 percent and be hampered by all those aforementioned items. It wouldn't be easy.

All that said, there's nothing wrong with owning mutual funds, so long as they're low-cost index funds. Stock screening is the best way to find great stocks, but sometimes you might only find a few stocks you really love, and you might not yet be confident enough in your stock-picking ability to put large dollar amounts in them. Index funds are great in that situation, because owning average stocks is better than owning no stocks.

I like Vanguard and Fidelity Spartan index funds because they're cheap. (I'm not keen on Fidelity *Advisor* funds, though. The "advisor" who sells them to you collects a big commission.) *Exchange-traded funds*, or ETFs, are even better if you're investing large dollar amounts all at once. Consider Vanguard's Viper ETFs. Read up on asset allocation, and be sure to mix some small-company funds and some international ones in with your stock holdings.

There are a couple of relatively new types of index funds that try to improve on the performance of existing ones. One type uses promising signs such as the amount of money a company pays its shareholders in dividends to weight the stocks, rather than just using company size. Wisdom Tree Investments offers funds of that type. Another relatively new type of fund uses *rules-based trading*. Instead of having a fund manager pick stocks or blindly following an index, these funds reshuffle the portfolio every so often to include stocks with the most promising attributes, such as low share prices relative to their profits. That's kind of like stock screening. PowerShares Capital Management offers funds of this type.

These funds are useful for when you have cash and don't have good stock ideas, but to capture spectacular returns we need to find great stocks. Let's look at some other people who want to pick stocks for you instead of letting you screen for them yourself.

Wall Street Analysts

Analysts are people who are paid by investment companies to research companies with the goal of determining whether their stocks are good buys. *Buy-side analysts* work mainly for mutual funds, hedge funds, pensions, and other money-management companies. They make recommendations on which stocks their employers should buy for the portfolios they manage. Buy-side analysts have little interest in recommending stocks to the public, because they're not paid to do so. If you read a news story about a stock that says that a certain analyst now thinks it's worth buying, you're probably reading the opinion of a sell-side analyst.

Sell-side analysts work mostly for investment companies that offer brokerage services. Their job is to come up with stock recommendations that the firms' brokers can use when advising their account holders. Sell-side analysts aren't shy about letting the general public in on their findings. In fact, they distribute their research to data collectors, who use it to publish consensus estimates and opinions that show what all the analysts who cover a particular stock think, on average, about its prospects. When people talk about following analyst recommendations, they mostly mean sell-side analysts. Their recommendations are the ones that are available to most investors.

In theory, analysts should come up with great stock picks. They don't have other day jobs to attend to. Stock picking is their day job, so they have a vast amount of time to devote to it. They also have big research budgets to work with. That means that, unlike most of us, they can spend their days visiting companies around the world and speaking with the people who run them and the customers who buy from them. They use these visits and conversations to develop detailed estimates of how much money the companies will make this year and next year. They use those estimates, in turn, to calculate target prices—share prices they think the stocks will fetch a year or two from now. If an analyst's target price is well higher than the stock's current price, the analyst will rate the stock a *buy*. If the two numbers are pretty close, the analyst will call the stock a *hold*. If the target price is lower than the current price, the stock might get rated a *sell*.

Investors can access these recommendations anytime they like on financial Web sites. They can also use stock-screening software to search for stocks that carry an average recommendation of buy or strong buy. (*Strong buy* means that analysts strongly recommend a stock, not that you should pound your keyboard extra hard while placing an order to buy it.) Think about it: Financial firms spend all that money on research, and the fruits of that spending are free for the taking. You don't have to spend a dime to put Wall Street's top researchers to work making recommendations for your portfolio.

But there are two problems. First, analysts are susceptible to bias when making recommendations. The firms they work for provide services for the same companies whose stocks they cover. For example, when a company wants to issue to new shares to raise capital, it hires an investment firm to help sell those shares to the public. That's a lucrative business for investment firms. Analysts receive bonuses that depend in part on the total revenues collected by their firms, whether for brokerage services or new-share-issuance services. So an analyst who places a sell recommendation on a company runs the risk that that company won't use their firm for other services, and that their bonuses shrink as a result.

Several studies over the past decade have shown that affiliated analysts—those who cover stocks for which their firms provide other services—tend to be more optimistic in their earnings estimates and less accurate in their buy recommendations. A few high-profile cases of analyst abuse (see Chapter 17 for an example) have resulted in greater scrutiny on the link between firms' research departments and other service-providing divisions. Analysts are therefore probably more cautious today about allowing bias to creep into their work, but the potential still exists.

The second problem with analyst recommendations is more of a deal breaker than the bias issue. They don't work. Investors who simply purchase stocks that have heaps of buy recommendations are unlikely to be pleased with the results. One exhaustive study of the subject published in 2004 in the *Journal of Finance* looked at more than 50,000 analyst recommendations made between 1985 and 1998. It found the predictive ability of those recommendations to be statistically insignificant.

Let's not write off analysts altogether. Their work is immensely useful, but perhaps not for the reasons they intend.

Buy recommendations might not be instructive, but changes in recommendations are. Studies show that investors can find great stocks by paying attention when analysts suddenly turn sweeter on a stock, especially when that happens to stocks in particular industries. That's the subject of the Rising Expectations stock screen strategy covered in Chapter 18.

Earnings estimates don't always prove accurate, but you can put wrong ones to work for you. As noted earlier, companies that exceed analysts' earnings estimates come reporting time are well worth a look by investors. Companies that beat earnings and sales estimates are particularly attractive. For more on why, read about the Surprise, Surprise screen strategy in Chapter 14.

It's not easy to publicly disagree with an opinion that nearly everyone else holds. When analysts issue earnings estimates that stand far away from the herd, studies show they're more likely to be right. Investors can use that tendency to find great stocks. That's the subject of the Bold Is Beautiful screen covered in Chapter 17.

Analyst recommendations are great for something else. I like to use them as a gauge of public perception. When running screens for value stocks—companies that are unpopular at the moment but that look likely to turn things around—I often eliminate from the results companies with average analysts' recommendations of buy or strong buy. That's because I want value stocks to have little popularity left to lose.

Stockbrokers

I like the word *stockbroker*. It tells you exactly what someone does for a living. A broker helps you buy and sell something in exchange for a commission. Sometimes brokers offer advice on what you should buy and what you should sell. A stockbroker does that with stocks, naturally.

That sounds like a valuable service. Instead of going through the trouble of learning about stocks for yourself, you can simply pay someone a fee to pick good ones for you.

Actually, the traditional stockbroker has all but disappeared. Today's stockbrokers can be divided into two main types. There are the ones that want to be called consultants, even through they're salespeople. And there are the ones who are mostly phone reps. They perform vastly different jobs but share one thing in common: They're unlikely to help you find good stocks.

Consultants

The first type of stockbroker goes by names like financial consultant, account executive, investment advisor, and retirement specialist. These brokers work for full-service investment firms like Merrill Lynch, Morgan Stanley, and AG Edwards. Ask what they do for a living and they'll tell you something like, "I take a consultative, planning-based approach to helping clients preserve and grow wealth." The consultant wants you to know that he's not interested in merely selling you a stock. He wants to learn about your "total financial picture" so that he can help you develop a long-term strategy.

When I was 20, I was hired as this type of stockbroker. I hadn't yet finished college. A big, reputable financial firm gave me a job as an associate financial consultant. The *associate* part meant that I was to be mentored by a senior financial consultant, the idea being that I would learn from a seasoned pro how to advise investors. My mentor, in return, was paid on the commissions I generated.

I was thrilled to have the job. I had a passion for learning how to pick good stocks. What better way to learn than as a stockbroker for a well-known firm?

I soon learned that picking stocks has nothing to do with being a stockbroker. Financial firms don't want to be responsible for an army of stockbrokers coming up with individual stock recommendations. So brokers are given a list of approved stocks to choose from. The stocks are hardly undiscovered gems. They're simply ones that analysts have given buy recommendations. We've just seen how helpful those recommendations are.

Brokers are paid according to the commissions their clients generate, not according to how well their clients' stocks do. Reputable firms like the one I worked for are pretty careful to make sure their brokers don't *churn*—flip clients in and out of stocks merely to generate heaps of commissions. Still, a broker has little incentive to tell his clients to hold stocks for a long time, even though that's the best way to invest in them.

Mostly, though, stockbrokers don't recommend stocks, even the ones their research departments select. That's because their firms prefer that they sell mutual funds. Mutual funds are the perfect products for stockbrokers. They carry enormous fees—much larger than stock commissions. Also, mutual funds outsource the job of picking good stocks and bonds. Firms like that, because by outsourcing the stock picking they outsource some of the responsibility if things go wrong. Also, when their brokers don't have to spend time choosing investments, they have more time to sell.

Recall that all those mutual funds have different fees. They also pay brokers different amounts to sell them. One fund might pay a broker 5 percent and another only 3 percent. Index funds with no sales charges—the only ones you should buy—don't pay brokers anything. That makes it hard for a broker to recommend funds based on their investment prospects and not on their fees, especially when there are monthly commission targets to hit.

Also, mutual fund companies have their own salespeople, whose job it is to convince stockbrokers to sell their funds, and not the competition's funds. They're called *wholesalers*. To accomplish their goal, they take brokers to nice lunches and ballgames, and they host contests with prizes for brokers who sell the most of their funds. It's awful to think that someone's nest egg is going into a particular mutual fund because their broker wanted to win a set of golf clubs, but it happens all the time.

Some of the brokers I worked with really did seem to want to do a good job for their clients. But I don't think they're given the tools, experience, or incentives to do so. It's nearly impossible to be an advocate for an investor when your pay increases as the investor loses money to fees. And it's just as difficult to learn how to pick good investments when you're paid according to how much you sell and not how much you know.

I was an awful stockbroker, by the way. I tried my best at a couple of firms and collected loyal customers along the way, but my commissions were always under target. I couldn't get the hang of selling mutual funds. Inevitably during my sales pitch, a customer would ask why he or she shouldn't just buy a fund with no sales charge instead of one with a 5 percent charge. I never had a good answer for that. To me, asking someone whether they want to pay a big sales charge or no sales charge is like asking whether they want a vanilla ice cream cone or a kick in the pants. I'd take the ice cream.

Phone Reps

You don't have to worry about being misled by the other type of stockbroker. The phone rep type doesn't recommend anything. They work for discount brokerage houses and, while they carry the same securities licenses as the other type of brokers, their job is simply to place trades for the few customers who don't yet place them online, and to handle customer service inquiries. In most cases they're specifically forbidden from giving investment advice.

Some brokers, by the way, are a mix of the two types. Some firms offer cut-rate stock trading, but try to steer customers with big cash balances toward expensive mutual funds. And some firms let their brokers recommend no-load funds for clients by having them work off a matrix of predetermined recommendations. That's just for mutual funds, though. Most stockbrokers today are neither allowed to nor able to help their customers pick great stocks.

Pundits

A pundit is someone who issues opinions in exchange for pay or publicity. They differ from journalists in that journalists defer to outside sources for the opinions they present in their stories. Pundits are their own sources. Often, they're experts.

Be careful about which pundits you listen to and how you use their advice. Not all of them are equipped to pick good stocks, and the ones that are often become victims of their own popularity.

Some pundits simply go on television programs and issue strong recommendations on the story stocks of the day. That's an easy ratings grabber, but investors end up with a wealth of contradictory opinions on Google and Apple and little advice about how to find the next Google or Apple.

Pundits who really know their stuff have two things working against them. First, their stock picks are in high demand, so these pundits come under pressure to make too many of them. Some have television programs where they issue a dozen or more recommendations a day. They might have the talent, experience, and strategies to pick great stocks. But I don't think they can pick a dozen of them a night, or even one a night. They can probably pick one great stock each month or maybe one each week, but that doesn't make for a daily television program. As talented as some stock pickers may be, the few gems they identify become diluted in a sea of ho-hum stocks that are just filling airtime.

The second factor working against pundits is that, as they become more popular, more people follow their advice right away. That drives up stock prices before you can buy. A stock that's recommended at $20 on an evening program might fetch $22 by the time you're able to buy shares the following day. If a 5 percent upfront fee on a mutual fund is unconscionable, a 10 percent premium to follow a pundit's pick is no bargain, either.

Company Bosses

The bias here is obvious. A company's boss isn't the right person to tell you whether you should buy shares of the company. I've spoken with many of them and I've never had one say, "Sell my stock now if you know what's good for you." Not only are they always positive, they're also often convincing. They got to be the boss for a reason, remember.

Better to let the bosses speak with their personal share purchases and not their words. Studies show investors who track such insider buying can profit handsomely, but only if they know which buys are the best ones to follow. That's the subject of the Follow the Leaders screen detailed in Chapter 19.

Friends and Relatives

I know: Your work friend Harry knows plenty about stocks, and he always picks great ones. And if you had only followed his advice on that last one, you would've made a fortune.

Still, be careful about following his advice on his next pick. Friends and relatives often hear about their stock picks from some of the sources already listed. It does little good to hear about a stock from Harry if he heard about it from his stockbroker who only recommended it because it's on the buy list at his firm.

The other problem with following stock advice from friends and relatives has to do with human nature. People like to talk only about their successes, because their successes make them look smart. (The opposite is true about what people like to hear, by the way. Your story about your recent promotion is nowhere near as entertaining to your friends as the one about how you threw a parking ticket onto the ground in disgust, then slipped on it, fell onto the dozen eggs you were carrying, and watched your pocket change roll into the sewer.) So Harry might wait until he's up a few points on a stock before he tells you all about it. Or, he might go into great detail about the stock he bought that doubled in price but forget to mention the three that flopped.

Forget about what friends and relatives are buying. You can find out what everyone is buying using a stock screener. Often, the first public sign of good news for a company is a rise in its share price. Share price momentum, remember, is one of the most powerful predictors of impressive long-term gains, provided you look for it the right way. See how in Chapter 12 on the Buy High, Sell Higher screen.

You're probably the best stock picker you know. Maybe you already know plenty about finding great stocks, and maybe you don't. But the knowledge can be filled in and the experience can be gained. What makes you great for the job is that you don't have any of the weaknesses facing the people we just covered.

Unlike mutual fund managers, you're not forced to buy hundreds of stocks to meet legally imposed diversification rules. You can buy just the few stocks you feel great about and, if need be, invest the rest of your money in index funds.

Unlike analysts, you don't have to worry about alienating potential customers if you snub the wrong stock. Also, you don't have to focus a disproportionate amount of your research time on giant companies. Feel free to look for young growers.

Unlike stockbrokers, you have no incentive to put your money in high-fee investments, or to buy and sell stocks frequently. You have an incentive to keep your fees as low as possible and find great stocks to hold for years.

Unlike pundits, you're not under pressure to come up with heaps of stock picks every week in order to attract viewers or readers. Search for stocks when you feel like it and spend plenty of time looking into the ones you like most.

You're best off on your own if you want to find great stocks, and a stock screener is the best tool for the job.

Besides, You're Probably Already Screening

If you buy stocks, you're probably already screening. That's because you're probably already basing your choices on company characteristics, like P/E ratios.

It makes sense, then, to take a methodical approach to making sure you're looking for the right clues, which is what the strategies in this book are about. It also makes sense to expand your search field from just the few companies you're able to compare in your head to the thousands you can scan using a computer.

Even if you don't own individual stocks, you might be stock-screening without realizing it. Let's say you own index funds and you just picked this book up to see what those stock pickers are talking about, but have no plans to be anything but a passive investor. Sorry, but you're already stock screening.

Suppose you own the Vanguard 500 fund. Recall that it tracks the S&P 500 index, which, in turn, follows America's 500 largest companies ranked by market value, more or less. (The index contains a few companies incorporated outside of the United States and it excludes companies that don't have sufficient trading liquidity.) You might consider your stake in the fund akin to owning a position in the broad stock market. In fact, it's similar to running a stock screen that looks for the country's largest companies. There are many thousands of American companies whose stocks you can buy, but you're screening for just the largest 500. Not only that, but the S&P 500 index gives the most weight to the big companies and the least weight to the small ones.

That's not helping your returns. Small-company stocks, remember, tend to outperform large-company ones over long time periods. *Efficient markets* proponents acknowledge as much by building the small-company effect into their stock-pricing models. You could earn far better returns over long time periods by simply buying a broader index fund. But you still wouldn't be passively investing. Chances are the index you choose will be weighted by market value, so that it will track the performance of big companies more than small ones. And it still probably won't include the entire stock market.

There's no truly passive index fund because there's no way to truly invest in the entire stock market. The best you can do is invest in an approximation of the market. I think you're better off reducing that vast universe of stocks by looking for attributes that tend to produce larger stock returns.

Just because you can beat the stock market, though, doesn't mean you should try. Isn't stock picking risky?

Stock screening only makes sense if the rewards to searching for great stocks are substantial and the risks to doing it are reasonable. In Chapter 5 we'll look at the risks involved in picking individual stocks. We'll also look at the risks of not picking them.

Chapter 5

The Rewards Outweigh
the Risks

S tocks are risky. That's true of individual stocks you pick for yourself and stocks you hold within a mutual fund that are picked for you by the fund manager or index methodology. Also, bonds are risky. Bank savings accounts are risky, too. So are certificates of deposit, precious metals, and the cash you hold in your wallet.

All financial instruments hold some form of risk. Some that seem safe based on one type of risk are anything but safe based on another. Let's look at the types of risk investors face, and then see where stock-picking stands.

Capital Risk

Capital risk is the risk that the value of your investment goes down. Some investments have virtually no capital risk. U.S. government bonds are guaranteed by the faith and credit of the government. That means that the government's ability to make good on your bonds is limited only by the government's ability to take money from you in the form of taxes to make its bond payments. Bank certificates of deposit are guaranteed by the Federal Deposit Insurance Company, a government agency. It doesn't collect tax payments, but it does collect mandatory insurance premiums from banks.

Both U.S. government bonds and CDs are virtually free of capital risk, so long as you hold them until maturity. Sell a CD early and you may be penalized. Sell a bond before maturity and you'll sell it at the going rate investors are willing to pay, which may be higher or lower than what you paid.

Stocks, of course, carry capital risk. They carry two types, really. There's *market risk*, or the risk that the entire stock market could decline in value, bringing your stocks down with it. And there's *issue-specific risk*, or the risk that the market does alright but you choose stinkers.

Judged on their capital risk alone, stocks are a risky investment. Note, though, that the capital risk involved in holding stocks can be significantly reduced if you hold good stocks for a long time, and if you hold a diversified portfolio of stocks. More on diversification in a moment.

Liquidity Risk

Liquidity risk is the risk that when it comes time to cash in your investment, there aren't enough buyers. It's different from capital risk, which is the risk that the buyers you find won't want to pay as much as you want them to pay. Liquidity problems arise when you can't find buyers, period. When that happens, sometimes your investment takes a long time to sell, and sometimes you're forced to sell at a sharply lower price in order to generate interest. You can reduce the liquidity risk in the stocks you search for by including a demand that they have ample average daily trading volume.

Currency Risk

Currency risk is the risk that, although your investments may do well and although you may be able to sell them without a hitch, the money you sell them for won't be worth as much relative to other currencies. If you're American and you load up on Mexican stocks, for example, and the value of the peso declines relative to the dollar, the dollar value of your stocks will decline, too. That's true regardless of whether you hold *ordinary* shares—ones listed on foreign exchanges—or dollar-denominated versions of those shares that trade in the United States.

For Americans, currency risk applies to U.S. companies, too, except maybe for companies that don't do business outside the United States and for Americans who don't plan to travel outside the United States to spend any of their stock profits. The value of the dollar has fallen sharply relative to currencies like the euro in recent years. And while there may be more than one reason for that decline, the U.S. government's recent inability to restrict its spending to the amount it collects in taxes surely hasn't helped. If the United States continues to run big budget deficits, the value of the dollar may continue to decline. That means that even if your U.S. stocks do well, you shouldn't expect them to fund leisurely trips through Europe in your retirement. Load up on U.S. stocks, by all means. But put some of your money in foreign companies, too.

Inflationary Risk

Here's where stocks actually look less risky than, say, bank CDs. Inflationary risk is the risk that the return on your investments fails to outpace inflation. *Inflation* is an economic term for a general rise in prices. Inflationary risk may sound like the kind of abstract financial concept that doesn't apply to you, but it might be the biggest risk you face over long time periods.

It's not enough to grow your pile of money between now and when you retire. Money is only as valuable as the amount of stuff it can buy. If your bank CD pays 3 percent a year in interest but prices in general rise by 4 percent a year, you're losing wealth. In fact, you're losing more than the amount by which you fail to beat inflation because you also have to pay taxes on your 3 percent return. That might not sound like a big loss, but remember how powerful the compounding effect of interest over long time periods is? It's just as powerful when it's working in the wrong direction. Low-return, *safe* investments like savings accounts, money markets, CDs, and U.S. government bonds carry heaps of inflationary risk. They might gradually increase the account value listed at the bottom of your monthly statement, but they'll do little to increase the amount of things you can buy.

Stocks are the best inflation-fighting investment going. Not coincidently, they're also the best tool for building wealth over long time periods.

Too-Old-to-Enjoy-It Risk

This factor rarely gets included in discussions of risk. I think that's a mistake. A 7 percent annual return combined with a healthy savings rate may help you beat inflation and gradually grow wealth so that you can stop working at 65 and enjoy yourself. But statistically speaking—sorry if this is a bit of a downer—you'll have a little more than a decade left to do so. Just as money loses value when it can't buy as much, it loses value when you don't have enough time to enjoy it. Investors must consider the risk that, if they don't take steps to maximize their savings rates and responsibly boost their returns today, they'll grow old long before they grow wealthy.

Suppose you're 35, have $20,000 to invest, and can afford to add $6,000 a year. Suppose, too, that you're not one of those annoying people who find their work pleasurable—if you had just $1 million today you'd leave your job, draw a $50,000-a-year income, and spend your days pursuing a proper mix of sloth and tomfoolery. You understand that stocks are the best place for your long-term savings, so you buy an S&P 500 index fund. Let's ignore taxes by assuming the money is in a tax-deferred retirement account, and let's assume the S&P 500 will do as well in coming decades as it has done over much of the past century, returning an average of about 10 percent a year before inflation.

It will take you more than 26 years to reach your goal of $1 million. But you won't really have reached it yet, because inflation will have eaten up some of the purchasing power of your portfolio. Assuming that inflation averages 3 percent a year while you invest, you'll have to work another eight years to amass $1 million in today's dollars. You'll be 69 by then.

A few great stocks in addition to your S&P 500 fund can make a world of difference. Boosting your annual returns by three percentage points, for example, will win back the eight years lost to inflation, leaving you blissfully unemployed at 61 rather than 69. You can also grow wealthy sooner by starting to save earlier or putting away more each year. But pursuing a few extra percentage points in your returns early on is akin to pursuing many extra years of not having to schlump to work every day, or at least, not having to worry about money while you do.

Back to our original question. Is stock-picking risky? Like index investing, it subjects you to capital risk but can fight inflationary risk. And it's better than index investing for reducing your too-old-to-enjoy-it risk.

A portfolio of a handful of stocks is subject to wider price swings than a portfolio of many stocks, but that can work for you or against you. Financial advice-givers often make it sound as though you can't possibly be too diversified. I think you absolutely can. If you own every stock, you can't possibly outperform the stock market. And although that won't make you poor, a couple of extra percentage points on your annual returns amounts to more than bragging rights or numbers at the bottom of an account statement. They translate to an earlier retirement, a more comfortable retirement, or both. I see that as a compelling reason to pick stocks.

It seems inconsistent to me that no one calls a pizza shop owner reckless for sinking his worth into a single business, but investors sometimes view owning a handful of businesses by owning individual stocks as too risky. Business ownership carries rewards that more than compensate for its risks. That's even more true when you can have your choice of thousands of businesses already up and running, and can buy your way into their profits without having to show up each morning to make pizzas.

The notion that stock picking is risky, and that ordinary investors are somehow not equipped to choose the businesses they want to own, has been crafted over the past 50 years. In my days as a stockbroker, I was struck by the contrast between customers of mine in their 70s and 80s who wouldn't dream of doing anything but investing in good businesses with strong profits and reliable dividends, and customers in their 30s and 40s who wouldn't dream of trying to do that for themselves.

This idea that stock picking is beyond our capability, I'm convinced, isn't owed so much to economists and math models as it is to the financial products industry carefully cultivating the idea. All those billions of dollars sitting in mutual funds generate ever-larger fees each year, while money invested in great individual stocks enriches only their owners.

Not only *can* you pick great stocks, you should. The rewards of finding them greatly outweigh the risks of looking for them. And you can shift the odds in your favor if you use three things: a stock screener, a good screening strategy, and careful research after your screen produces its results.

There are many strategies to choose from, but a limited number of reliable winners. Let's look at how to recognize them when you see them.

Chapter 6

Telling Great Screening Strategies from Not-So-Great Ones

I was a terrible mutual fund salesman, as I've told you. But let me try to talk you into a bad stock-picking strategy just the same.

The Pitch

Have you heard about the XYZ investment strategy? It's simple. Look down a list of stocks in the S&P 500 index—America's 500 largest companies, more or less. Buy ones that start with the letters X, Y, or Z. That's it.

Start thinking about how you're going to spend all those profits. If past performance of the XYZ strategy is any indication of future returns, it's sure to be a success.

Okay, there hasn't been any *past performance* per se. That's because the strategy is new. We'll have to rely for now on *back testing*. Back testing involves using a computer and a big database of stock information to tell how a strategy would have done had we been following it over the years. I checked the returns to my strategy in early March 2007. Over the prior year those XYZ stocks—there were nine of them—gained an average of 15 percent. That's 7 percentage points more than the average for all 500 stocks we started with.

I see you're not calling your stockbroker yet to place buy orders. Perhaps you think the one-year results were just luck. Very well, consider this: Over the past three years, my alphabetically disadvantaged stocks gained 48 percent. That's eight percentage points better than the 500 stocks. And over the past five years they gained a stunning 95 percent, trouncing the 500-stock return of 67 percent. Plenty of talented money managers wish they had results like that to boast about.

Past Returns Sometimes Lie

On Wall Street, recall, the numbers sometimes lie. The numbers cited above are accurate, but my XYZ strategy is nonetheless a sham. Your intuition probably told you that. It wouldn't make sense to invest in companies just because their names start with particular letters. The performance numbers may have surprised you, though. They were strong over the past one, three, and five years. That's as much evidence as mutual funds offer when they advertise their past success. Anyone can have a good year or two, but longer-term outperformance suggests more than just luck.

In fact, there's usually more than luck involved. Long-term, market-beating returns advertised by mutual funds, investment newsletters, stock alert services, and the like are usually attributable to one of three things:

1. *A reliable stock-picking strategy.* We'll look at some of those later in the book.
2. *A skilled stock picker.* More often than not, that's someone who does a good job of following a reliable stock-picking strategy.
3. *A financial parlor trick.* These can make anyone look like a genius stock picker.

You probably encounter the most common varieties of financial parlor tricks all the time. Here are a few.

Self-Fulfilling Prophecy

Stock alert services sometimes cause frenzied buying in the stocks they recommend. The shiftiest ones—the kind that send unsolicited picks via e-mails designed to outwit spam filters—usually focus their recommendations on small companies with thinly traded shares in hopes of causing a big share price jump. Larger, subscription-based services sometimes have so many members that they can send even shares of medium-sized companies higher in the minutes following a recommendation.

At the time of this writing, one of the most prominent of these services is GorillaTrades.com. It charges $600 a year for a subscription. The company won't say exactly how many subscribers it has, but it boasts members in 36 countries and it advertises relentlessly on CNBC. That's not cheap, so I'm guessing the ads must be paying off in big subscriber growth. GorillaTrades says it screens 6,000 stocks nightly for the "14 technical parameters for explosive growth." Just before subscribing, you'll have to check a box that says you understand the material on the site is "for general informational purposes only" and isn't "intended as investment . . . advice" or "an endorsement . . . of any company." That's odd, since the service consists principally of "GorillaPicks" and trigger, target, and stop-loss prices.

Such services tend to move the share prices of the stocks they recommend. It's not difficult to generate a good stock-picking record when you can do that. Unfortunately, many people who subscribe to the services don't see those returns. Sometimes the stock prices jump before they're able to buy. Worse, sometimes they get caught up in the excitement and buy just when everyone else is starting to sell.

Survivorship Bias

Here's an easy way to be a stock market genius. Call 800 people. Tell half of them that the stock market is going up tomorrow and the other half that it's going down. (Perhaps now would be a good time to mention that this is illegal.) By the end of tomorrow, you'll have given prescient advice to 400 people. Call them and tell half the market will rise and half it will fall, same as before. Continue until you have 50 people with whom you've been right four times in a row. Tell these amazed folks that you'll be happy to predict more market movements—for a fee (again, illegal).

Today's mutual fund and hedge fund industries were all but founded on a strategy not too different from this one. They launch far more funds than they need, and select different investments for all of them. Underperformers get closed or merged into other funds, thereby erasing their performance histories. Winners get marketed. Ever wonder why you hear about so many funds with stellar histories, despite what the statistics say about most funds doing poorly? It's because the losers don't get talked about. Then they disappear. If you could make your losing investments disappear, you'd have numbers worth bragging about, too.

Data Mining

The parlor trick I used to create the XYZ strategy is called *data mining*. Data mining is the act of scanning a large database of changing information for two pieces of information that seem to move in relation to each other. Data points that change are called variables. The seeming link between two variables is called *correlation*.

Finding correlations isn't difficult. Every variable is correlated in some way with every other variable. It's just a matter of how strong the correlation is. Strong correlations aren't difficult to find, either. If the number of variables you're searching through is large enough, in fact, they're sure to turn up.

I used data mining to create the XYZ strategy in about 20 minutes. I didn't work off a hunch that those particular letters would do better than other ones. I used screening software to select all stocks that are members of the S&P 500 index and to display past returns for each. Then I downloaded the results to Excel, a spreadsheet program that makes poking and prodding big columns of data easy. I grouped the companies alphabetically by the first letter of their names, calculated average returns for each letter group and looked for the letters that had done the best. The numbers were good for G, H, O, P, V, X, Y, and Z. Then it was just a matter of deciding on which combination of letters sounds cool. HOG was a close second.

Data mining is the opposite of how most people come up with a good idea. Normally, they think about a problem, come up with a logical solution, and then research that solution to see if it's likely to work. "Some fertilizer might help my tomatoes," you might say. "Let me read up on the subject and talk to Larry down at the lawn and garden store." A data miner would randomly try, say, gardening with his left hand only, wearing a necktie while weeding, and any other variation he can think of until one corresponds with—produces, seemingly—healthier tomatoes.

Data mining in general is plenty useful. It helps drug companies develop new treatments by trying out millions of chemical combinations using computer simulations, and it helps economists improve life expectancies by looking for new ways to make sense of reams of measures of how people use their resources. Misused, though, data mining can help someone "prove" a relationship that doesn't really exist. Pity the gardener whose necktie really did seem to make his tomatoes healthier, while unbeknownst to him, it was really just a change in humidity. He might be in for years of overdressed horticulture before he realizes his mistake.

There are plenty of examples of advisory services that use data-mining to convince investors of their stock-picking prowess. One stock-picking service recently sent me a research piece boasting about the success of its return on equity screen. *Return on equity* is a measure of how efficiently companies use the things they own to generate profits. It's a useful measure, and we'll look more closely at it later. But this company said its return on equity screen had produced annual returns of greater than 80 percent. That's impressive for a single stock, but for a basket of stocks it's unheard of. I read on. It turns out the returns were over a five-year period, which isn't long enough to ensure they weren't just coincidence. Most important, the screen hadn't really compiled 80 percent-plus returns over that five-year period. Rather, the company had used a back-test to suggest that the screen *would* have returned that much.

It's easy to create a winning strategy if you can look back over the past five years and pick the variables that coincided with the biggest stock gains, just like I did with the letters in the XYZ strategy. It doesn't mean the strategy will work with real money, though.

Back testing is useful for finding good stock-picking strategies, but it has to be done the right way. When researchers back-test, they make adjustments for factors that are known to produce big stock returns. We'll see how they do that in a moment. Also, they compile the results over longer time periods. More than two decades is best. The best screen strategies I've seen have consistently topped the broad market's returns by 5 to 13 percentage points a year. If you choose stocks from a basket of winners like that, the chances of your next stock being a great one—one that doubles in price in two or three years—improve dramatically. But be wary of investment services that claim to be producing entire baskets of stocks that beat the market by 50 percent or 80 percent a year.

Five Signs of a Winning Strategy

The strategies you'll want to incorporate into your own stock screens— that is, the combinations of clues you'll want to look for—should have five main characteristics:

1. They've worked well in the past (*correlation*).
2. There's a good explanation for why they've worked (*cause*).
3. There are no other, hidden explanations (no *lurking variables*).
4. They're practical. That is, the strategies won't keep you staring at a trading screen for eight hours a day and won't generate so many commissions that your returns get eaten up.
5. They can be translated into the language of stock-screening tools.

Correlation and Cause

The past performance of a stock-screening strategy should be impressive over a long time period. But that past performance must also come with a good explanation as to why it occurred. That is, correlation should come with a cause.

The investor who relies on performance at the expense of a good explanation figures the numbers don't lie. But he risks being lured by back-tested results and data mining into a strategy that doesn't work as well in the future as it seemed to have worked in the past.

The investor who settles for a good explanation but doesn't bother checking into past performance faces a different problem with similar results. He might end up following a strategy that sounds logical but fails to produce returns.

I gave you an example of a strategy with good numbers but no logical explanation—my XYZ strategy—so let's look at one with a good explanation but no numbers to back it up. Cash is a good thing for companies to have. It makes them financially strong. They can use cash to pay dividends, reduce debt, pay for growth initiatives, and more. So companies with lots of cash lying around ought to be winners, right? They're not. Studies show that companies with too much cash tend to underperform the broad stock market. Managers tend to use big cash balances to make ill-advised purchases that expand their influence, but not their stock prices. Researchers have a name for that tendency: *empire building*. Too much cash lying around, it seems, means companies have run out of good growth projects, or have forgotten that they're supposed to return excess profits to shareholders through dividends and other means, or both. A mountain of cash is a bad sign, but that's just the opposite of what intuition might have told you.

Lurking Variables

Watch out for lurking variables. They might lead you to believe a correlation exists for one reason, when really it exists for another. A common example used to illustrate lurking variables is the correlation between ice cream consumption and violent crimes. In months when people eat more ice cream in the United States, the number of violent crimes increases. Before you call for a ban on pints of Ben & Jerry's Chunky Monkey, though, you should know that there's a lurking variable: hot weather. People eat more ice cream when it's hot. They also commit more violent crimes when it's hot, because when it's cold and the days are short, people spend more time at home.

The most likely lurking variables in stock strategies are things like company size and valuations. Suppose I test the stock performance of companies that make their own television commercials rather than hiring an advertising agency, and I find that they outperform the broad market by two percentage points a year. Do I have the makings of a winning strategy? Unlikely, unless there's a good explanation for why home-grown ads would drive stock prices. More likely, companies that make their own ads are too small to hire outsiders for the job, and small companies produce better stock returns than large ones, so my result came from a lurking variable: company size.

Most of the strategies we'll look at in this book have already been tested for the presence of lurking variables. Researchers do this using a tool you're already familiar with: the Fama/French three-factor model (see Chapter 2). Recall that the model was designed to use a company's past volatility, size, and price/book ratio to calculate its expected stock return. It doesn't do that perfectly because it fails to include all of the vast number of clues that predict fat stock returns. But the model is still plenty useful. It's great for testing strategies to see whether their past returns are merely due to the size effect (small companies do better), the value effect (low P/B ratios do better), or both. When a strategy has produced impressive long-term returns, includes a good explanation for those returns, and has passed a test for lurking variables, you might have a winner. But you need two more things first.

Practicality

A strategy that has you trading from your house all day every day is difficult to follow if you enjoy human contact, the outdoors, or having a reason to put on pants in the morning. Frequent trading also raises fees and taxes. Fees and taxes on their own aren't the most important consideration. If the returns are high enough, they're worth it. But just make sure you take them into consideration.

None of the strategies in this book require frequent trading.

Screenability

A great strategy or clue does you little good if you can't put a number on it or plug it into a stock screener. For example, money managers often say it's important for a company to have a good *moat*. A moat in this sense is something that keeps competition low. It could be a patent or a strong brand. You can't screen for moats. You have to do one of two things instead. You can translate "moat" into something a screener can understand. For example, companies with strong moats tend to be able to charge higher prices because they don't have much competition. That keeps their profit margins—the portion of sales they keep as profits—high. You can screen for high profit margins. The second thing you can do with a moat is to save it for use in the research you perform on the handful of companies that come out of your screen. That's a perfect time to consider promising company attributes that you just can't screen for.

Other Not-So-Proven Strategies

Before we move on to the stock-screening tools and the things you can screen for, I thought you might like to check out some other stock-picking strategies of dubious value to investors. Some lack cause, others lack correlation, and others are based on too little data. One of them, the second one, was created by a money manager named David Leinweber to illustrate the pitfalls of data mining.

Football Follies

Buy stocks whenever a team from the original American Football League wins the Super Bowl. Sell stocks whenever a team from the original National Football League team wins. Since 1967, the Super Bowl indicator has been stunningly accurate, correctly predicting the market's direction more than 80 percent of the time.

Bengali Butter

Buy stocks when butter production in Bangladesh increases. Between 1983 in 1993 a 1 percent increase in production predicted a 2 percent gain for the S&P 500 index. A 1 percent decrease in butter production predicted a 2 percent decline for the index.

Short Skirts

Buy stocks when short skirts are in fashion. Sell stocks when skirts lengthen. Bold fashion is a sign of general confidence, which, in turn, is good for the economy.

Headaches

If the stock market falls, invest in aspirin companies. Financial stress causes headaches and can lead to surging pain-killer sales.

Make-Up

Sell stocks when lipstick sales increase. During times of economic uncertainty, consumers turn to purchasing inexpensive but comforting items like lipstick rather than luxury items.

Elections

Buy stocks in the year before a presidential election. The stock market has suffered only three down election years. Since World War II it has never had a negative pre-election year. In order to get reelected a sitting president will boost spending or cut taxes in an election year, spurring the economy and driving share prices higher.

Part Two

TOOLS AND CLUES

Chapter 7

How to Use a Screening Tool

The perfect temperature for brewing coffee is between 195 and 200 degrees Fahrenheit. I'm pretty sure of that. I run something of a coffee laboratory out of my kitchen. I use terms like *roast curve, dosing,* and *extraction.* I don't yet say *cupping* instead of *drinking,* but I'm getting close.

Let's say you're in the market for a new coffee maker and you want one with the right brew temperature. (We'll assume you haven't yet discovered that low-tech brewers like press pots and vacuum pots are better than drip coffee makers, and that pressure brewing with an espresso-style machine is better still.) You go online and start searching through models, all the while looking for the following clue:

Brew temperature in degrees Fahrenheit is between 195 and 200.

The Three Parts of Any Clue

The three main elements to stock screening are all contained in your coffee maker clue. There's the variable (brew temperature in degrees Fahrenheit), the relationship (between), and the value (195 and 200).

The Variable

The variable is the piece of information you're making a demand on. Note that the variable just given contains both the data point you're looking for (brew temperature) and the unit of measurement (degrees Fahrenheit). Screeners sometimes have hundreds of variables to choose from. We'll look at many of them in the next chapter. Since there are so many variables for users to choose from, they're generally divided into categories and subcategories. Often, this is done with a pull-down menu that branches out. So a user looking to make a demand on price/earnings ratios might click on *ratios,* then *valuation,* and then *P/E.* Usually there will be a few types of P/E ratios to choose from, each using a different measure of earnings—but more on that in the next chapter. More variables make for a better stock screener, generally speaking.

The Relationship

This is sometimes called the *operator* or *condition.* It's how the value you're about to specify relates to the variable you just chose. Examples include greater than ($>$), less than ($<$), equal to ($=$), not equal to ($\neq$) or a combination of those, like greater than or equal to ($\geq$). Some screeners include "between" as one of the variables, and some require you to express "between" in a two-step process. In the case of our coffee maker clue, you'd turn it into two clues, like this:

Brew temperature in degrees Fahrenheit $>$ 195.

Brew temperature in degrees Fahrenheit $<$ 200.

The screener you use might offer more relationships, depending on how the screener handles things like comparative clues, and whether it has an equation builder. We'll look at those in just a moment.

Value

This is what you want your variable to be equal to, not equal to, between, and so on. It is sometimes called the *base*. Whereas the variable and relationship are usually selected from lists of available choices, the value field may be a free entry field where you type in a number. Or it may change from free entry to a pull-down menu, depending on the variable you use. For example, if there was such a thing as a coffee maker screener, and if you chose *brew temperature* as your variable, you might get a free entry field for the value, allowing you to type in any number you like. If you chose color as the variable, you might get a pull-down menu for the value with a choice of only black and white.

Let's forget about coffee makers now and search for a real stock clue. The variable we'll search for is operating margin. We'll look into its significance in the next chapter. For now, just know that it measures the portion of a company's sales that it keeps as profits after taking out for manufacturing and operating costs. Companies with high margins show that they are able to charge high prices for their goods and services, keep their own costs down, or both. To look for operating margins greater than 10 percent, the clue would look like this:

$$\text{Operating margin (\%)} > 10$$

Is that a good operating margin? I don't know, because I don't know what kind of company we're talking about. Some companies, like giant, deep-discounting retailers, sacrifice margins in order to bring in a flood of customers and ring up plentiful sales. Others, like posh jewelry stores, would rather keep prices high and deal with fewer customers but capture larger profits from each one. Neither of these approaches is necessarily better than the other. Both a deep discounter and a specialty story can have impressive or lousy operating income (sales times operating margin). They just go about generating them differently. Better to search for companies whose operating margins compare favorably with other companies in the same business.

Comparative Clues

Let's look for operating margins that are above their industry averages. Stock-screening tools treat such comparative searches in two main ways.

The first is by listing industry averages as separate variables so you can select them as your value, like this:

Operating margin (%) > Industry average operating margin (%)

The second way is to offer the industry compare function as a relationship choice. That looks something like this:

Operating margin (%) Top % in industry = 50

In this case, instead of choosing the "greater than" sign as the relationship, the user chose "Top % in industry." Sometimes this pull-down menu branches out, so you'll click "Top % in" and then be given a choice of "industry," "S&P 500," "all," and so on, so that you can search for stocks that compare favorably to indexes and to the entire database, too.

Formula Builder

All of the stock screeners we'll look at include operating margin as something you can screen for. It's a pretty basic variable. But let's pretend it's not a commonly used measure and that the screener you're using doesn't have it. You might be able to make it. All you need is a formula builder. A formula builder introduces basic arithmetic signs for addition (+), subtraction (−), multiplication (∗) and division (/), and lets you combine two or more variables to form other variables.

Operating margin is calculated by dividing a company's operating income by its sales for the same period. Suppose your screener offers both operating income and sales as variables even though it doesn't have operating margin. You can still search for operating margin with the formula builder, like this:

(Operating income / sales) > 0.15

Note three things about the previous clue. First, we've put parentheses around the calculation we want to do first, before we search for the entire clue. Second, we've changed 15% to 0.15, because now we're making a ratio, instead of using one that has already been turned into a percentage. Third, we're back to using a plain ole' number as the value rather than an industry comparison. Most screeners don't offer industry averages for variables you create.

A formula builder is among the most useful features a stock screener can have. It greatly increases the number of variables you can screen for. It also allows you more flexibility in your comparisons. For example, suppose your stock screener is the type that makes industry comparisons like this:

Operating margin (%) > Industry average operating margin

But instead of looking for operating margins that are merely above their industry averages, you want to look at those that are at least half again as high as their industry averages. If a particular industry's average operating margin is 10 percent, you want companies with operating margins of 15 percent or greater. With a formula builder, you can build that clue like this:

Operating margin (%) > (1.5 * Industry average operating margin)

More than One Solution

Sometimes there's more than one way to build a clue. If you want to look for companies with operating margins that have grown over the past year, you might have two choices. They look like this:

Operating margin growth (%) > 0
Past year operating margin (%) > Prior year operating margin (%)

Which you choose in this case makes no difference. If you can't find one way to search for a clue, look for another.

Clue Order

When you're using more than one clue, as you'll likely be doing most of the time, enter them in the following order.

Start with the Must-Haves

If you wouldn't consider investing in companies with negative profits, there's no point in including them in your search. The first clue you add should be that profits are greater than zero. Be careful about starting with too many must-haves. For example, a company might have temporarily negative profits due to a one-time accounting charge for a lawsuit settlement, but its sales might be growing nicely, and having the lawsuit out of the way might make the company worth a look. We'll look for companies with positive profits in the strategies covered in this book, but I wouldn't consider that clue a must-have in every situation.

I generally look for two must-haves in my screens: a minimum amount of sales and a minimum average trading volume. By looking for companies with at least, say, $50 million or $100 million in sales over the past year, I include small companies but exclude the smallest start-ups. And by looking for average daily trading volume of, say, 100,000 shares I focus on companies that are easy to buy and sell because plenty of other buyers and sellers are available to take the other side of the trade.

Add the Main Themes

If you're running a screen for accelerating sales growth, now's the time to add those clues. For example:

Five-year average sales growth (%) > 20
Three-year average sales growth > Five-year average sales growth
Past-year average sales growth > Three-year average sales growth

End with the Nice-to-Haves

Whether you make extra demands depends on how big of a list of companies your main-theme clues produce. If you've reduced a 9,000-company database to just 12 stocks, you might want to skip the nice-to-haves and start right in on your research. If you have 65 screen survivors, you might want to further reduce the list. You can either make your main theme clues stricter, or you can add a nice-to-have—say, a smidgen of share price momentum.

Saving Recipes, Presaved Recipes

I call a collection of two or more clues a *recipe*. It might take you a few minutes to input all your clues. If you create a screen you'll want to run again, many screeners will let you save your recipe. That way, the next time you want to run it you can do so with one click, often by selecting your saved recipe from a pull-down menu. Many screeners also include a list of presaved recipes. These have been created by the company that made the screener. It helps if there's a write-up explaining what the recipe is trying to look for, and why. Make sure these recipes are based on the elements of a good stock-picking strategy that we covered in Chapter 6.

Running the Screen

After you add your clues, just click the button that says "execute," "calculate," "find stocks," or something like that. Some screeners automatically reduce the list of screen survivors each time you start to add a new clue. It's a good idea to run the screen each time you add a clue or two so that you can monitor how quickly your list of survivors is shrinking.

Fiddling with the Results

Once you've created a list of screen survivors, you can simply jot down the names and research them on your own. But it's easier to create a report of the names, which most screeners will let you do. Usually you'll be able to choose which data points you want to include in your report. So even though you haven't screened for, say, low price/earnings ratios, you can add P/Es to your report to use in your post-screen research.

Many screeners will let you reorder the list of survivors that comes up. So if low P/Es are important to you, you can order the companies from lowest to highest P/E. Spreadsheet programs such as Microsoft Excel can do far more sorting and fiddling than stock screen programs. For that reason, many screeners include an export function that can turn your list of screen survivors into an Excel file, or another type of file.

There's More

I've left out a few things, but you can learn those as you go. As you tinker with the screening tool of your choice, you'll discover that it's useful for more than just running searches based on your strategies. For example, you can search for a single company by ticker symbol in order to simply create a report on that company with heaps of data. Or you can search for all companies that are members of a particular industry, export the list to Excel, and use it to calculate industry averages—to see what the average car maker's stock has done over the past year, for example.

You know how things go with software. It gets updated every so often. Five years from now screeners will likely have new features, and they might present old features in slightly different ways. The broad strokes will be the same, though.

Chapter 8

The Screeners

The perfect stock-screening tool doesn't exist, but if it did it would have these six attributes:

1. *It would be easy to use.* You wouldn't have to read instructions to get started.
2. *It would let you search for anything.* If you can think of a company attribute, and if the data for it are out there, the perfect stock screener would let you search for it.
3. *It would let you tinker with the results.* You'd be able to sort the stocks that come up on your screens anyway you like, make reports on them, download those reports, and so on.
4. *It would be stable.* The software would never freeze up on you.
5. *It would never make mistakes.* The data you search through would be reliable.
6. *It would be free.* Paying for stuff isn't as fun as not paying for stuff.

Screeners that (Mostly) Deliver

In this chapter we'll look at the screeners that come closest to delivering on all of these things. These are listed alphabetically. I'll tell you what each screener's strong points are and what its weaknesses are. I'm covering only screeners that range in price from free to $100 a month. That's a reasonable price range, I think, viewed next to the prospect of finding great stocks. Also, I'm excluding screeners that are only available to institutional customers and not to individual investors. After looking at all the screeners, I'll give my top recommendations.

American Association of Individual Investors ($21 a Month)

This site, www.aaii.com, is plenty useful for those with an interest in stock screening. The American Association of Individual Investors (AAII) is a nonprofit organization, but it charges for access to the best goodies on its site. Memberships start at $29 a year and allow you to browse the site. Stock screener access costs $247 a year for nonmembers and $198 a year for members.

One helpful feature of the site is that it tracks performance figures for dozens of stock-screening strategies. Some of these are designed to mimic renowned investors, and others just look for particular mixes of clues. The results only go back to 1998, and the first several years of results are back-tested figures rather than ones that were produced live. Also, the performance figures don't reflect the rigorous set of adjustments that academics usually make to account for known predictors of big stock returns we covered earlier in the book, such as the size effect and value effect. Still, the site's stock-screen horserace is interesting, and it will only prove more interesting the longer the performance is tracked. Also, the site has something of a workshop feel, which means you won't be dodging flashing, punch-the-monkey banner ads while you read up on stock screening.

The AAII Stock Investor Pro is the only disk-based stock screener covered in this section. AAII mails you the install disk and monthly disk updates, plus you can download weekly updates. The software will run on most Windows-based computers.

The screener is among the most capable you'll find. It includes a plentiful list of variables and a formula builder so that you can create new variables. You'll find 50 stock screens preloaded onto the screener, along with descriptions of what they look for. You can save your own screens and download your list of screen survivors to Excel for further sorting. Also, the screener includes something called Stock Notebook, which allows you to pull up pages of financial information on any screen survivor you want to investigate. It operates like the stock snapshot pages on a financial Web site, except it's offline.

All these features will cost you more than your yearly fee. You'll also have to invest some time to figure out how the screener works. This isn't a just-toss-the-manual-aside-and-dig-in type of tool. But with a read-through of the instructions and some practice time, you'll be fine.

AOL Money and Finance (Free)

This is a good example of the easiest-to-use type of stock screener, but also the least flexible one. Users are given a clean Web page (money.aol.com/investing/stockscreener) with a simple stack of 20 or so pull-down menus. There's no need to choose your own values to go with the variables you screen for. That's done for you. So rather than search for, say, P/Es below 15, you select "10.0 to 25.0" from the pull-down menu labeled "P/E."

The data implementation could be better. At the time of this writing, many of the variables were displayed to two decimal places in the screen results, but with zeroes for both those decimal places: 1.00, 2.00, 3.00, and so on. That appears to be due to a faulty rounding process, combined with a faulty stick-a-couple-zeroes-on-the-end process. The rounding won't matter so much with big numbers such as, say, one-year sales growth. It renders smaller numbers such as dividend yields and price/sales ratios nearly meaningless, though. That is, a stock with a price/sales ratio that reads "1.00" might really be a 0.6 or a 1.4. That's a big difference; one company is more than twice as expensive as the other.

There are some limited choices for post-screen research. You select a couple of companies for a side-by-side comparison, for example. There's no option to download your screen results. AOL offers about eight preprogrammed screens, but with no explanation for why they work. With names like "Stocks Set to Double Earnings," a little explanation is probably warranted.

This screener is designed for stock investors who value ease of use more than advanced functionality, but readers of this book should probably look elsewhere.

Marketwatch (Free)

This screener, too (marketwatch.com/tools.stockresearch/screener), is simple to use but a bit on the basic side. The choice of fundamentals to screen by, for example, is limited to two variables: price/earnings and market value. There are only around seven screen variables in total.

Screen results can't be downloaded. Display options are few. One plus: The screener offers intraday prices, so you can screen for stocks that are, say, up big today. There are more capable free screeners out there.

Morningstar (Free or $15.95 a month, Free Two-Week Trial)

This screener is unique (screen.morningstar.com/stockselector.html). The layout is simple and clean, with pull-down menus and check boxes. You'll have no trouble figuring out how to run a screen. What sets the screener apart is its use of proprietary measures. You can select stocks by "Morningstar stock type," for example. Choices include "classic growth," "hard assets" and "distressed." You can also select for "Morningstar equity style box." If you've seen Morningstar's mutual fund reports, you know how this works. Stocks are classified on a tic-tac-toe grid with small, medium, and large on one axis and value, core, and growth on the other.

You can screen using a dozen or so basic variables. Rather than enter your own values, you select them from the pull-down menus, which doesn't allow for much flexibility. Alternatively, you can search for stocks with certain Morningstar stock grades, A through F, for three characteristics: growth, profitability, and financial health. Running a screen, then, can be as simple as checking three boxes to look for stocks with straight As. Once you have a list of screen survivors, you can rank them by assigning scores of zero through 10 to a series of variables. For example, if you give "growth" a 10 and "low P/E" a zero, you can expect your screen survivors to be ranked according to growth rates with little regard for P/Es.

Morningstar has set up nine preprogrammed screens. Each comes with a quick explanation of what it looks for and why.

This screener doesn't offer the flexibility needed to run most of the searches in this book. But for a user who doesn't want to be bothered plugging in variables and trusts Morningstar's ranking system to identify good stocks, it's an excellent tool.

Morningstar also offers a beefed-up screener as part of its premium Web site membership, which costs $15.95 a month or $145 for a year. The screener offers far more criteria and a list of preprogrammed screens.

MSN Money (Free)

MSN offers two stock screeners. The first (moneycentral.msn.com/investor/finder/customstocksdl.asp) consists of 11 simple pull-down menus with limited choices. For example, you can search for price/earnings ratios that are "as high as possible" or "as low as possible."

The company's Deluxe Screener (moneycentral.msn.com/investor/controls/findpro.asp) delivers far more capability. It might require a quick software download, depending on whether your Web browser already speaks its language. There are more than 100 variables to screen with. The layout follows the standard field-operator-value layout, so you can search for measures in any value range you like. You can also look for, say, price/earnings ratios that are below their industry averages or their own five-year averages.

The screener allows you to search for what MSN calls Advisor FYI alerts. These are variables, operators, and values all in one: "gross profit margin increased," for example. You can also search for stocks graded A through F by MSN's "StockScouter" system for any of a dozen or so characteristics such as valuation and risk expectation.

Users can save searches and download the results to Excel. Elsewhere on its site, MSN lists more than a dozen one-click screens that run outside the screener.

It's an excellent screener, considering that it's free, and it will allow you to run many of the searches in this book. One minus: There's no formula builder, so you can't combine two or more variables to make new variables.

SmartMoney.com ($5.95 a Month, Free Two-Week Trial)

As of the writing of this book, I was also writing SmartMoney.com's Stock Screen column. That means I spend plenty of time using the site's stock screener. It also means I'm biased. But it's a fine screener.

Three screeners in this chapter are similar in appearance and use: this one, the MSN screener, which we've already looked at, and the Yahoo screener, which we'll get to in a moment. The SmartMoney.com screener is the best of the three. It offers a choice of screening variables comparable to the MSN screener. It lacks an equivalent to MSN's letter grade system to search for stocks that, say, get an "A" for financial strength. If you're reading this book, though, you'll likely prefer to specify your own measures of financial strength, which you can do with this screener. Also, the SmartMoney.com screener costs $6 a month, while the MSN one is free, but for that money you also get access to several other tools on the site and to premium columns. These include the Stock Screen column, which several times a week looks into a stock that one of the screener's 20 or so preprogrammed screens recently produced to determine whether it's worth buying.

The screener offers a few other things the MSN screener lacks. Chief among them is a formula builder. There are also some useful display options once you've generated a list of screen survivors. For example, you can view the stocks as thumbnail charts, which allows you to compare recent share price momentum among eight or ten companies at a glance.

This screener will run many of the strategies presented in this book and can come close enough on most of the others. For $6 a month it's a great choice for someone who wants a combination of power and ease of use.

Validea ($29.95 a Month)

This site specializes in guru screens. You can use stock screens designed to mimic the stock-picking techniques of one of the researchers (Joseph

Piotroski) and three of the money managers (Warren Buffet, Peter Lynch, Martin Zweig) I've based strategies on in this book.

Like AAII, Validea keeps a running scorecard on its site showing how the screens have done. The numbers only go back to 2003, but they're not produced by mere back testing. They're actual performance numbers of portfolios based on the screens that are rebalanced monthly. The company has even launched a money management business based on the screens.

Validea's stock-screening capability comes in three varieties. First, you can simply have the site show you 10 or 20 screen survivors based on whichever guru strategy you choose. Second, you can rank gurus—tell the screener that you're kind of into one guru but way into another—and have it produce stocks based on those preferences. Third, you can use that same process but overlay screen criteria on the end. So you can search for, say, stocks that both the Buffet and Lunch strategies would have produced, but make sure they're all in a particular industry and all have price/earnings ratios below 20.

One other cool feature on the site: Plug in a ticker symbol, and it will tell you which guru strategies approve of the stock you're looking at.

The site costs $29.95 a month, or $269.95 if you pay for a year up front. It won't run most of the strategies we'll look at in this book, but it's nonetheless worth a look for someone with a particular interest in guru screens.

Yahoo Finance (Free or $13.95 a Month, Free 30-Day Trial)

I'm skipping the exclamation point that's meant to appear on the end of "Yahoo" because, well, that kind of Internet-company-name rule-breaking is a little 1999 for my tastes. But I'm no less enthused about the company's finance site (finance.yahoo.com).

Yahoo offers two stock screeners. There's a free one, which is the last of the triplets—the set of remarkably similar tools that includes the MSN and SmartMoney.com screeners. There's also one that includes real-time stock pricing that runs $13.95 a month. The price falls to $9.95 a month if you pay for a year in one shot.

First, the free screener. It includes many of the features of the others, but doesn't have MSN's proprietary measures or SmartMoney.com's formula builder and thumbnail charts option. You can put together a decent screen or choose from a couple dozen preprogrammed results. You can also download your results to Excel and save screens for later use.

The advanced screener is part of Yahoo's Portfolio Tracker software, which offers charts, scrolling news, and real-time price updates. I find both screeners a bit too buggy for regular use. For me, they produce screen artifacts (little pictures that stay where they're not supposed to) and some freeze-ups. I know almost nothing about making software, but both the Yahoo and SmartMoney.com screeners rely on a programming language called Java. It's powerful, but tricky to implement, I'm told. SmartMoney.com seems to have fared better with it than Yahoo for now. MSN's screener is based on something called ActiveX, which works nicely with Microsoft browsers.

To Yahoo's credit, its finance site is one of the best going for researching stocks after you run screens. The pages are clean and thoughtfully laid out, and Yahoo populates them with data from many of the best sources, rather than simply the cheapest ones. I'd skip the screener but use the site.

Zacks Investment Research (Free or $24.95 a Month, Free Two-Week Trial)

Zacks offers three stock screeners. There's a free one on the company's Web site (zacks.com/research/screening/custom/index.php) that allows you to screen for a few dozen variables using number inputs but not industry comparisons. By paying $14.95 a month for a premium membership, you get an extra criterion to screen for: the Zacks Rank. That's a simple 1 to 5 rating that suggests whether you should buy or sell each of about 4,000 stocks. Zacks boasts that its top-ranked stocks have consistently beaten the market over the past couple of decades.

The company also offers a far more powerful screener called the Research Wizard. It's a stand-alone program rather than one that runs inside a Web browser. It offers a long list of screener variables, a formula builder, preprogrammed screens, an export function, and more. It's a great program, but a pricey one. Access starts at $1,000 a year.

The Research Wizard includes a built-in back tester, so if you're wondering how a particular strategy would have performed over the past five years, you can check. You can also see which stocks would have survived your screen at some past point. (Read up on data mining and survivorship bias in Chapter 6 to understand the limitations of back testing.) You can also print out one-page company reports on any of your screen survivors.

The Zacks Research Wizard is probably easier to use than the AAII screener. It also includes a screener within a screener—you can click the EZ Screen button to access a simple list of pull-down menus if you find the full screener overwhelming at first.

Best Screeners

In my opinion, here are the best screeners in the following categories.

Top Free Screener: MSN

It's capable enough, considering the price.

Top Almost-Free Screener: SmartMoney.com

You get a formula builder, some extra options for displaying your results, and access to the Stock Screen column for ongoing reading on the subject. The software is powerful and the $6 a month won't break you.

Top Not-Nearly-Free Screeners: AAII, Zacks

These will do everything you want, but they take longer to learn and they cost a bit extra. The AAII program requires regular updates with disks, while the Zacks screener handles that automatically.

Chapter 9

Where the Numbers Come From

Most of the stock-screening metrics you'll base searches on are what I like to think of as baked goods. Consider the price/earnings ratio. It's made up of three raw ingredients: share price, earnings, and number of shares outstanding. (It's really the price/earnings-per-share ratio.)

One of those ingredients without the others doesn't tell you much about a stock. You can't begin to consider whether a company with $35 million in earnings last year has inexpensive shares unless you know how many shares the company has been split into and how much each of those shares costs.

In the next chapter, we'll learn which baked goods you should use to search for profitable companies, growing companies, well-managed companies, and so on. In this chapter we'll see where the raw ingredients that make up those baked goods come from. You can skip ahead, of course, but understanding the ingredients will help you in three ways. First, you'll have a better feel for baked goods like *return on equity* if you know where its ingredients, earnings and equity, come from and what they measure. Second, some screeners let you bake your own goods using a list of raw ingredients and a formula builder. I want you to know how to do that. Third, by knowing where all the ingredients come from, you'll be better equipped to do further research on your screen survivors.

Data providers are companies that fetch raw ingredients from their original sources and stuff them into databases, both as-is (earnings) and as baked goods (price/earnings). Some of these companies work only behind the scenes, so their names might not be familiar to you: Hemscott and Capital IQ, for example. Others make front-end tools like stock screeners in addition to providing data. Examples include Zacks Investment Research, covered in Chapter 8.

Data providers get their raw ingredients from three sources. The financial information comes from companies themselves. The stock-trading information comes from exchanges. The estimates and recommendations come from Wall Street analysts.

Source 1: Companies

In the United States, all companies whose shares we can buy and sell must issue regular reports of their financial condition, so long as they have at least 500 investors and assets of $10 million or more. These reports show how much money these companies made, spent, invested, borrowed, and so on. Companies must issue annual results within 90 days of their fiscal year end and quarterly reports within 45 days of their fiscal quarter end. (Big companies must report faster.) By *fiscal* year and quarter I'm referring to the accounting year a company chooses for itself. It may or may not coincide with the calendar year. For example, some store chains choose to end their fiscal year on January 31. That's so that all activity associated with the Christmas selling season, including January's returns, exchanges, and gift-card redemptions, hits in the same quarter.

In the United States, companies report their financial information to the Securities and Exchange Commission (SEC), a government agency that regulates the stock market. Before the mid-1990s, companies created paper reports and mailed them to their shareholders and to the SEC. Stockbrokers got their information from printed sources, such as Standard & Poor's *tear sheets*—one-page summaries of financial information that went into a binder. Stock screening existed only in a limited and expensive form; a few companies mailed disks to customers each month with updated financial information on a select group of companies.

Today companies file financial information via Edgar. It's not a person. It's a system for collecting and distributing company reports. *Edgar* stands for Electronic Data Gathering, Analysis, and Retrieval. Companies file their quarterly and annual results on the system, and may file reports in between quarters if they do something important to investors, such as buy another company or replace a key executive.

The combination of the Internet and Edgar has made stock screening cheap, powerful, fast, and easy. Data providers pull their information off Edgar, pretty it up, and send it on to their customers. You can access Edgar filings directly if you like. That's useful if you want to take a close look at a single company. (Edgar filings are more reliable and usually more informative than financial Web sites, but they take longer to look through.) Links to SEC filings are provided on the stock quote pages of many financial Web sites, Or, you can go to SEC.gov and look for a link to Edgar.

The government loves form numbers. Just as they call your income tax return your 1040, they call a company's quarterly and annual reports its 10-Q and 10-K, respectively, and that's how Edgar lists them. The three most important sources of financial information contained in each 10-Q and 10-K are the income statement, balance sheet, and cash flow statement.

Income Statement

The income statement tells you whether a company operated at a profit or a loss for the quarter. A typical income statement starts with sales on the top line and ends with earnings on the bottom, taking out for various costs and charges along the way. (Hence, sayings like, "The company anticipates excellent top-line growth" and "We want to improve the bottom line.") Some companies report things differently. Banks, for

	53 Weeks Ended February 3, 2007	52 Weeks Ended January 28, 2006
	(In $ thousands, except per-share and statistical data)	
Sales	5,318,900	3,091,783
Cost of sales	3,847,458	2,219,753
Gross profit	**1,471,442**	**872,030**
Selling, general and administrative expenses (2)	1,000,135	598,996
Depreciation and amortization (2)	109,862	66,355
Stock-based compensation (3)	20,978	347
Merger-related expenses (4)	6,788	13,600
Operating earnings	**333,679**	**192,732**
Interest expense (income), net	73,324	25,292
Merger-related interest expense (4)		7,518
Debt extinguishment expense	6,059	
Earnings before income taxes	**254,296**	**159,922**
Income tax expense	96,046	59,138
Net earnings	**158,250**	**100,784**
Net earnings per common share basic (5)	1.06	0.87
Weighted average shares outstanding basic (5)	149,924	115,840
Net earnings per common share diluted (5)	1.00	0.81
Weighted average shares outstanding diluted (5)	158,284	124,972

Figure 9.1   Gamestop Income Statement.

example, don't generate sales as such. They usually break their income statements into two parts: one that starts with interest received (e.g., loans) and subtracts interest paid (e.g., savings accounts), and another that starts with noninterest income received (e.g., cash machine fees) and takes out for noninterest expenses (e.g., marketing). A few financial Web sites and stock screeners recognize the difference between an income statement from a manufacturer and one from a bank. Most just shoehorn everything into the same format—a manufacturer one. Let's look at a simplified income statement in Figure 9.1. Don't panic. It's not complicated, and I'm going to go through it fast, like a nurse giving a flu shot.

Income statements do *not* measure the money a company receives and pays each quarter. (That's the cash flow statement.) They measure the new business a company writes up and the new expenses it takes on, regardless of whether the money has changed hands yet. Also, they use tricks that break down big, one-time purchases into small, quarterly pieces. You can read all about why companies do this in Chapter 20 on the Accrual to Be Kind screen strategy. For now, just know that the income statement is of particular interest to stock investors who want to know whether a company is making good operating decisions, while the cash flow statement is of particular interest to lenders who want to know how much cash is going into the till as a result of those decisions.

We start with sales at the top. They're sometimes called *revenues*. They represent the total dollar amount of all the goods or services a company sold during the statement period. Companies generally record sales once the good has been delivered or the service performed. Sometimes, income statements start with *net sales*. That just means sales have already been adjusted for things like rebates and returns.

Next, we take out for *cost of goods sold*, here labeled simply *cost of sales*. For manufacturers, this includes the cost of raw materials and labor. For resellers, it includes the wholesale prices they pay for the goods they resell. For service companies, it includes costs incurred in providing services. This line contains only the cost of goods sold during that period, not the cost of goods that haven't yet been finished or shipped.

The first measure of profit is called *gross income* or *gross profit*. It's the portion of sales left after subtracting the cost of goods sold.

Now we take out for *corporate costs,* or SG&A, which stands for *selling, general, and administrative expenses*. These include advertising campaigns, salaries, bonuses, headquarter's electricity bills, and so on. Expenses that can be linked to specific product sales are recorded in the same period. Those that can't are broken down proportionally throughout the year.

Another important expense that's not listed on our table: *research and development (R&D)*. This is the amount companies spend to come up with new products or keep existing ones fresh and competitive. Retailers don't often spend on research, but drug and technology companies do. See the Tomorrow's Breakthroughs screen strategy in Chapter 15 to learn how to use R&D spending to find bargain stocks.

Big, one-time purchases of things that will produce sales in the future, like new plants and equipment, aren't deducted on the income statement. Instead, they're broken down into quarterly charges over the projected useful life of those items. That's to keep companies from reporting huge losses when they make investments, followed by huge gains when they don't. Those charges are called *depreciation* if the item is tangible and amortization if it's intangible, such as a patent or brand. Depreciation and amortization charges on an income statement represent just that period's usage of those items. (Remember, the income statement is designed to tell a story about current operations, not to count money that changes hands.)

Notice that Gamestop has subtracted for the cost of its stock-based compensation—employee stock option grants and such. That's a relatively new accounting requirement. Companies used to issue employee options without deducting for their cost, treating them as free money, when really, options often get converted into shares, and an increase in a company's number of shares makes existing shares less valuable.

Gamestop has also taken out for costs related to a recent merger. After that we come to another measure of profit: *operating earnings*, sometimes called *operating income* or *operating profit*. It's what's left from gross income after taking out for SG&A, R&D, depreciation, and amortization. Sometimes it's called *EBIT*, or earnings before interest and taxes. (You might have heard the term EBITDA, which is generally not listed on a company's income statement. It's like EBIT only it also ignores charges for depreciation and amortization. We'll look at how to use it in later chapters.)

Next, we subtract for the interest a company pays on the money it has borrowed. Sometimes companies report a net figure here that offsets interest paid on loans with interest collected on investments. There are also entries for more merger-related costs and for the repayment of debt.

That gives us *pretax income*. Investors may judge a company by its pretax income if they think tax events are distorting aftertax income. For example, a company may be using past losses to reduce its taxes this year, but will run out of such credits before next year.

Next we take out for *taxes*. Companies don't subtract taxes they've actually paid here, but rather, taxes they've set aside to pay.

We've come to *net earnings*, also called *net income* or *net profit*. Sometimes you'll see an entry for *net income from operations,* followed by *extraordinary items* to add or subtract from net earnings. These are charges or credits due to unusual, nonrecurring events, like damage caused by a freak storm or money won in a lawsuit. Companies have a fair amount of leeway in deciding what's extraordinary and what's not. Beware of companies whose extraordinary charges begin to look too ordinary, serving as annual excuses for why profits are not what they should be.

Notice that Gamestop then offers its earnings per share in both *basic* and *diluted* form. Diluted earnings per share make assumptions about how the share count will increase once options and such are converted into shares. Generally speaking, you should use diluted earnings per share when deciding things like how expensive a company looks.

Net earnings are what's left from sales after subtracting all expenses and making all accounting adjustments. The earnings figure companies report on their income statements is called *GAAP earnings*, so named because it's calculated using generally accepted accounting standards published by the Federal Accounting Standards Board.

You can come up with a dozen or more ways to measure earnings by making simple adjustments to GAAP earnings. Stock screeners include many of these measures. One measure might exclude extraordinary items. Another might exclude employee stock-option expenses. (That measure was popular at the time of this writing, because the recent shift to expensing was skewing their year-over-year earnings growth.)

Sometimes you'll see a measure called *pro-forma earnings*. That's a measure companies report (or analysts calculate) when they feel that certain GAAP charges have distorted the story the income statement tells. Pro-forma earnings might pretend a merger that happened within the past year actually happened years ago, for example. When you use pro-forma earnings, pay attention to the adjustments that have been made, and make sure they're things that really tell a fairer story, and not just a rosier one.

The logical flow of information on an income statement helps companies and their investors see where problems pop up, if there are any. If sales are decent but gross income is too low, a company needs to find cheaper materials or labor. If gross income is okay but operating income is too low, the bosses might be spending too lavishly at headquarters. If depreciation and amortization charges chronically eat up too much of the profit, someone probably spent too much on investments in the past.

That's it for the income statement. Your flu shot wasn't so bad, was it? Good, because there are two more shots coming up. I'll make them quick, too.

Balance Sheet

The *balance sheet* records the value of things a company owns and the amounts it owes. Some of the items on a company's balance sheet are assets and debts that remain there a long time. Some items, like inventories, are just passing through, waiting to be converted into sales on the income statement.

Balance sheets show a company's financial condition on a single day: the last day of the reporting period. That's different from income and cash flow statements, which measure movement of money over the entire period. You can think of income and cash flow statements as movies filmed during the entire quarter or year and balance sheets as a snapshot taken on the final day.

For a company's balance sheet to be just that—in balance—two things must be equal. The value of assets must equal the *liabilities* (the borrowed portion) plus *equity* (the owned portion). If you've ever borrowed to buy a home, you'll understand this basic balance sheet equation. Your home is an asset. It's equal to the portion you own (equity) and the amount left on your mortgage (liability). See Figure 9.2.

We start by tallying assets, first current ones and then long-term ones. For balance sheet purposes, the cutoff between current and long-term is usually one year. So *current assets* are those that are expected to be converted into cash within one year.

Cash and equivalents is the first current asset. Equivalents are things like money market accounts.

Net receivables are the next current asset. This is money a company is owed for goods or services that it has delivered or provided but has not yet been paid for. Accounts receivable arise because companies extend credit to their customers.

Next you'll sometimes see *short-term investments*. These include stocks and bonds—things a company can sell quickly. (Don't think of *your* stocks as short-term investments, though.)

The last major current asset is *inventories*. This is the value of raw materials, nearly finished goods, and finished goods that a company will eventually sell.

Often there's an entry for *other current assets*. This is a catch-all for stuff that doesn't fit under the other descriptions. For example, a company

	February 3, 2007	January 28, 2006
	($ thousands)	
ASSETS		
Current assets:		
Cash and cash equivalents	652,403	401,593
Receivables, net	34,268	38,738
Merchandise inventories, net	675,385	603,178
Prepaid expenses and other current assets	37,882	16,339
Prepaid taxes	5,545	21,068
Deferred taxes	34,858	41,051
Total current assets	**1,440,341**	**1,121,967**
Property and equipment:		
Land	10,712	10,257
Buildings and leasehold improvements	305,806	262,908
Fixtures and equipment	425,841	343,897
Less accumulated depreciation and amortization	285,896	184,937
Net property and equipment	**456,463**	**432,125**
Goodwill, net	1,403,907	1,392,352
Assets held for sale		19,297
Deferred financing fees	14,375	18,561
Deferred taxes	5,804	
Other noncurrent assets	28,694	31,519
Total other assets	**1,452,780**	**1,461,729**
Total assets	**3,349,584**	**3,015,821**
LIABILITIES AND STOCKHOLDERS' EQUITY		
Current liabilities:		
Accounts payable	717,868	543,288
Accrued liabilities	357,013	331,859
Notes payable, current portion	12,176	12,527
Total current liabilities	**1,087,057**	**887,674**
Deferred taxes		13,640
Senior notes payable, long-term portion, net	593,311	641,788
Senior floating rate notes payable, long-term portion	250,000	300,000
Note payable, long-term portion	412	21,675
Deferred rent and other long-term liabilities	42,926	36,331
Total long-term liabilities	**886,649**	**1,013,434**
Total liabilities	**1,973,706**	**1,901,108**
Stockholders' equity:		
Preferred stock authorized 5,000 shares; no shares issued or outstanding Class A common stock $.001 par value; authorized 300,000 shares; 152,305 and 145,594 shares issued and outstanding, respectively	152	146
Additional paid-in-capital	1,021,903	921,335
Accumulated other comprehensive income	3,227	886
Retained earnings	350,596	192,346
Total stockholders' equity	**1,375,878**	**1,114,713**
Total liabilities and stockholders' equity	**3,349,584**	**3,015,821**

Figure 9.2   Gamestop Balance Sheet.

might have cash that it's restricted from using for now because of a contract. Gamestop has included *pre-paid expenses*, which are things like rent that has been paid in advance. It has also recorded the value of *deferred taxes*. These sometimes arise because a company has carried over a loss from a prior period to use against future income.

Add these items together and you get *total current assets*. Next let's look at *long-term assets*.

First are *fixed assets*, sometimes called *property, plants, and equipment*. These are tangible, income-producing items the company expects to continue owning for longer than a year. Fixed assets get depreciated on the income statement.

Next are *intangible assets*. These are nonphysical assets such as patents, copyrights, and brands. Such assets produce real profits because they allow companies to charge higher prices for their products. Sometimes you'll see a separate entry for *goodwill*. That's an intangible asset that arises when a company pays more than the net asset value for another company. Accountants have to make an entry detailing what exactly the purchasing company paid for. Goodwill is this entry. It can include assets as vague as good customer relations. Intangible assets get amortized on the income statement. In general, intangible assets a company purchases are recorded on its balance sheet, while those it develops internally are not.

Next are entries for the long-term portion of deferred expenses and fees. Sometimes there's an entry labeled *other long-term assets*, here called *other noncurrent assets*. This can include oddball items like the amount by which a pension plan is overfunded.

Add all those long-term assets to the short-term assets we tallied earlier and you get *total assets*. Next up are liabilities, starting with the short-term ones.

First are *accounts payable*. This is money a company owes for products and services received. Accounts payable are due in less than one year. *Accrued liabilities* are things like wages and rents that must be paid.

Next is *short-term debt,* also due in less than a year. Often this is money that has been borrowed against a line of credit. Lines of credit carry higher interest rates than long-term debt, so companies should use them only for short-term needs.

Other short-term liabilities might be listed separately or crammed together in one line. These include things like dividend and tax payments that are coming due.

Tally those items up and you get *total current liabilities*. Now we move on to long-term liabilities.

There's an entry for deferred taxes. Unlike the earlier entries for deferred tax assets, which represent a benefit waiting to be used, this represents taxes from a past event waiting to be paid.

Next is *long-term debt:* bank loans, bonds, notes payable to individuals, and so on. Then comes *other long-term liabilities*. These can include what are called capitalized lease obligations. Companies can avoid debt by simply renting their plants and equipment, but that still results in monthly payments. This entry treats amounts due on long-term leases as though they were a pile of debt today.

Sometimes you'll see an entry for minority interest. In cases where a parent company owns less than 100 percent of a subsidiary, minority interest represents the portion the parent doesn't own. So if a company owns 80 percent of a $1 billion subsidiary, $200 million is recorded as minority interest. That's because a company that buys an 80 percent stake in another company gets to record all of that company's assets on its balance sheet. Since it only truly owns 80 percent of those assets, minority interest makes the adjustment on the liabilities side.

Add all those long-term liabilities to the short-term ones we looked at earlier and you get *total liabilities*. Now let's look at equity.

Preferred equity is the amount of money a company has raised by issuing preferred shares. We're not covering preferred stocks in this book, but suffice it to say that they usually carry fixed dividend rates and function more like bonds than stocks.

Common stock here isn't the value of outstanding shares. (That's called market value.) Rather, it's the money a company initially raised by issuing shares. Here it's broken into a tiny *par value* and a larger amount for *additional paid-in capital*, which together represent the total amount investors paid for shares.

Accumulated other comprehensive income is another catch-all entry for gains and losses that haven't yet been realized, like amounts due for an underfunded pension or gains from investments.

Next are *retained earnings*. These are earnings a company doesn't pay out to shareholders as dividends, but keeps to reinvest into its business.

Add those items together and you get *total shareholders' equity*.

Add total liabilities to total equity and, if the accountants have done their job properly, you get a figure that's equal to total assets.

Two down, one to go.

Cash Flow Statement

The *cash flow statement* measures, well, cash. Flowing. It shows how much of it a company took in and paid out during the period. It cares nothing about telling a good story to stock investors or matching expenses with benefits in the same time period. It just measures cash. It's divided into three sections that correspond with the three ways companies get their hands on and spend cash: their operations, their investing, and their financing. See Figure 9.3.

First let's look at the cash flows from *operations*. There are a couple of ways companies can report this section. We're using the most common method, called the indirect method. It starts where the income statement left off, with net earnings. The idea is to undo many of the adjustments made in calculating net income in order to figure out how much real cash was produced.

Remember depreciation? Add it back in. Rather than breaking down big-ticket purchases into small, quarterly charges, we're going to subtract them all at once in a moment.

Next, we adjust for changes from one period to the next in the value of certain things listed on the balance sheet. These include current assets like accounts receivable and inventories and current liabilities like accounts payable. Adjustments here can be positive or negative. For example, a company's accounts receivable may have increased or decreased during a particular quarter.

Eventually we come to *net cash from operating activities*. Now let's look at investment activities. Note that we start over from zero rather than continue with what we have so far.

First, we deduct for *purchases of property and equipment*, also called *capital expenditures*. These are the big-ticket investments that get deducted in full on the cash flow statement rather than depreciated little by little.

	53 Weeks Ended February 3, 2007	52 Weeks Ended January 28, 2006
	($ thousands)	
Cash flows from operating activities:	158,250	100,784
Net earnings		
Depreciation and amortization	110,176	66,659
Provision for inventory reserves	50,779	25,103
Amortization and retirement of deferred financing fees	4,595	1,229
Amortization and retirement of original issue discount on senior notes	1,523	316
Stock-based compensation expense	20,978	347
Deferred taxes	(3,080)	(3,675)
Loss on disposal and impairment of property and equipment	4,261	11,648
Increase in deferred rent and other long-term liabilities	9,702	3,669
Increase in liability to landlords for tenant allowances, net	1,602	202
Minority interest		
Decrease in value of foreign exchange contracts	(4,450)	(2,421)
Changes in operating assets and liabilities, net of business acquired		
Receivables, net	2,866	(9,995)
Merchandise inventories	(118,417)	(91,363)
Prepaid expenses and other current assets	(21,543)	19,484
Prepaid taxes	52,663	9,069
Excess tax benefit realized from exercise of stock options	(43,707)	12,308
Accounts payable and accrued liabilities	197,306	148,054
Net cash flows provided by operating activities	**423,504**	**291,418**
Cash flows from investing activities:		
Purchase of property and equipment	(133,930)	(110,696)
Merger with Electronics Boutique, net of cash acquired		(886,116)
Acquisitions, net of cash acquired (including purchase of Game Brands, Inc.)	(11,303)	
Sale of assets held for sale	19,297	
Net cash flows used in investing activities	(125,936)	(996,812)
Cash flows from financing activities:		
Issuance of senior notes payable relating to Electronics Boutique merger, net of discount		641,472
Issuance of senior floating rate notes payable relating to Electronics Boutique merger		300,000
Repurchase of notes payable	(100,000)	
Purchase of treasury shares through repurchase program		
Repurchase of common stock from Barnes & Noble		
Issuance of debt relating to the repurchase of common stock from Barnes & Noble		

(Continued)

Figure 9.3 Gamestop Cash Flow Statement.

Repayment of debt relating to the repurchase of common stock from Barnes & Noble	(12,173)	(12,173)
Repayment of other debt	(9,441)	(956)
Proceeds from exercise of stock options	33,861	20,800
Excess tax benefit realized from exercise of stock options	43,707	
Net increase in other noncurrent assets and deferred financing fees	(2,609)	(13,466)
Net cash flows provided by (used in) financing activities	**(46,655)**	**935,677**
Exchange rate effect on cash and cash equivalents	(103)	318
Net increase (decrease) in cash and cash equivalents	**250,810**	**230,601**
Cash and cash equivalents at beginning of period	401,593	170,992
Cash and cash equivalents at end of period	652,403	401,593

Figure 9.3   (*Continued*).

Next we adjust for *investments*. These can be purchases and sales of other companies or securities like stocks and bonds.

That gives us *cash from investing activities*. Now let's continue to financing activities, starting from zero again.

Most of the entries in this section relate to the issuance or repayment of debt and the issuance or repurchase of shares. You'll also see an entry for dividends if the company pays them and proceeds from the exercising of stock options if any occurred. . . . Together those things give you *net cash from financing activities*. Now add the three figures from operations, investing, and financing, and you get the company's total change in cash and cash equivalents for the period.

That's it for the raw ingredients found on company financial statements. We'll mix many of these into useful measures in the coming chapters. Income statement ingredients will help us tell how profitable and well-run companies are. Balance sheet items will tell us how wealthy companies are. Cash flow statement measures will tell us how strong companies are. And of course, by comparing these items to a company's market value, we'll be able to tell whether its shares are expensive or cheap.

We have two more sources of raw ingredients to look at, but they're not nearly as involved as company financial reports.

Source 2: Exchanges

Stock exchanges sell information on how stocks trade to data providers. Among the pieces of information they sell are closing share prices, high and low prices for the day, and volume of shares traded each day. Data providers compile this information and use it to keep track of things like high and low prices for the past year and average trading volume over the past three months.

Most stock screener databases get updated once a day, usually at a time when the majority of users of those stock screeners are likely to be asleep. Some databases update price information continuously throughout the day, though. Often these screeners are designed for day traders, or investors who buy and sell stocks many times throughout the day for quick profits (or quick losses). This book focuses on strategies for long-term investors, so a screener that updates once a day is fine for our purposes.

Source 3: Analysts

Data providers poll analysts to collect their earnings and sales estimates and their recommendations—buy, hold, and so on. They then use this information to create consensus, or average, estimates and recommendations. They also report the number of analysts contributing to those opinions and how the opinions have changed in recent weeks and months.

Chapter 10

Things You Can Screen For

In this chapter we'll look at individual clues and what they say about companies. These are the clues made up of the raw financials we looked at in Chapter 9, and collections of these clues will make up the strategies explained throughout the rest of the book.

Most of these clues say good things about stocks. Some say indifferent but nonetheless useful things. If these measures are new to you, don't become overwhelmed by the number of them. You won't have to use all of them. The best strategies are based on just a few of them. You can skim through this section now and use it later while you screen as a reference.

Company Descriptions

These are mostly useful for selecting the universe of stocks you want to search through in your screen.

Ticker Symbol

The symbol a stock trades under is the ticker symbol. Use this if you want to run a screen for a single stock you're interested in researching, and then generate a report on that stock with all the data points you care to include.

Country of Domicile

This is where a company is headquartered. Use it to search for foreign stocks, but be aware that some companies base themselves in tax-friendly countries but do most of their business elsewhere. If you live in the United States and you want to buy foreign stocks to diversify a portfolio of mostly U.S. ones, it does little good to buy shares of a Bermuda-based company that collects 85 percent of its sales in the United States.

Sector

The sector is the area of the economy in which a company operates. Choices often include basic materials (e.g., oil drillers), energy (e.g., power companies), consumer cyclical (companies that make goods like motor homes that are sensitive to economic cycles), consumer non-cyclical (companies that make goods like food that don't react much to economic cycles), financials (e.g., banks), healthcare (e.g., drug makers), industrials (companies that make things for other manufacturers), technology (e.g., computer chip makers), and telecommunications (e.g., the phone company).

Use sector and industry (below) to run what are called top-down stock searches. Most of the screens discussed in this book are bottom-up searches, where you start by looking for attractive company attributes. Top-down searches are those where you start by identifying the area of the economy you want to invest in, and then look for attractive company attributes. Top-down searches are useful for investors who feel their portfolios are underweighted in an important area of the economy.

Industry

Industry is like sector, but much more finely divided. While *financial* might be a company's sector, *regional bank* might be its industry.

ADR Indicator

ADR stands for American depository receipt. That's a dollar-denominated version of a foreign stock that trades on a U.S. exchange. ADRs are generally easier to buy and sell than the corresponding ordinary shares that list on foreign exchanges. Note that ADRs carry essentially the same currency risk of ordinary shares. The ADR indicator is a yes/no choice that allows you to search for stocks that have ADRs, or exclude them.

Index Membership

Index membership allows you to search for stocks that are members of major indexes such as the Dow Jones Industrial Average or the S&P 500. This field is useful for following strategies that search for attractive stocks from within a particular index. See the New Dogs strategy in Chapter 16 for an example.

Number of Employees

Just like it sounds. There isn't much point to searching for companies with a minimum or maximum number of employees, but if the screener you use has a formula builder, you can create some interesting measures of productivity like sales per employee and profits per employee.

Analyst

This lets you search for stocks covered by a particular Wall Street analyst, just in case you find one you feel is particularly accurate or particularly inaccurate.

Auditor Opinion

Use this field to search for companies whose auditors have signed off on their financial reports, or those whose auditors have unanswered questions.

Share-Level Attributes

These clues describe stocks more than they do companies.

Share Price

Share price allows you to search for companies with minimum or maximum share prices. Major exchanges sometimes have minimum share price requirements for the stocks they list, so you might want to restrict searches to stocks that go for at least a few dollars a share to avoid delisting concerns. Share price is also useful with screeners that have formula builders. If, say, the price/sales ratio isn't offered, you can build your own using share price and sales.

52-Week High/Low Price

This is the highest or lowest price a stock has reached over the past 52 weeks. A stock's proximity to its 52-week high price is a useful measure of share price momentum, which is one of the most powerful predictors of future returns. See Chapter 12 on the Buy High, Sell Higher screen to learn how to use this clue to find great stocks.

Beta

Some investors view beta as an indispensable way to judge a stock's risk. I think it's overrated, and that there are better ways to judge a stock's risk. Beta is calculated using a statistical technique called *regression analysis*. The past relationship between two variables is used to predict their future relationship. In the case of a stock's beta, the stock price is one of those two variables and a broad index like the S&P 500 is the other. The index is assigned a beta of 1.0. A stock whose beta works out to, say, 1.5 is projected to be 50 percent more volatile than the index based on its performance during the calculation period (usually three to five years.) One with a beta of 0.7 is projected to be 30 percent less volatile. One with a negative beta tends to zig when the broad market zags. The idea behind beta is that low-beta stocks should perform less poorly than the broad market if the market tumbles. So you should hold low-beta stocks if you're worried about the stock market but want to stay invested. Again, I'm not convinced that beta is the best tool for the job of finding safe stocks. It tends to penalize young, fast-growing companies for stock volatility in past years, even if those companies have matured considerably. That can make the most attractive companies seem undesirable. And keep in mind that low volatility theoretically works both ways, reducing losses when the market falls but crimping gains when it rises.

Average Volume

The average number of a stock's shares that changed hands over the specified period, often 30 days. Some screeners let you choose the period. Average volume is one of those clues you can use in just about every screen you run. Stocks with decent average volume are easier to buy and sell and are less likely to drop sharply if someone places a big sell order. Look for average daily trading volume greater than 100,000 shares or so to ensure you're investing in companies with sufficient trading liquidity.

Outstanding Shares

Also called issued shares, they include common shares held by the public and restricted shares, which are shares held by company insiders who face restrictions in selling them. If you use outstanding shares in a search it will most likely be because you're converting a financial statement item to a per-share amount using a formula builder. Or, you might look for companies whose number of outstanding shares is falling, on the assumption that this is due to share repurchases. The best screeners include issued shares and repurchased shares as separate variables. See the New Dogs strategy in Chapter 16 for more on why share repurchases are important.

Diluted Shares Outstanding

Same as shares outstanding, only it assumes all convertible securities like options and convertible preferred shares have been turned into common shares.

Float

The total number of common shares available to the public. A company's float is equal to its outstanding share count minus its restricted share count.

Market Capitalization

Also called market value, this is the total amount it would cost to buy all of a company's outstanding shares at the current stock price. Market cap is calculated by multiplying stock price by the number of shares outstanding. When investors talk about small caps, mid caps, and large caps, they're referring to the size of companies' market caps. Just how small of one makes a company a small cap is somewhat subjective and changes over time with the overall value of the stock market. At the time of this writing I was using the $1 to $5 billion range of market caps for midcaps, with small caps falling below that range and large caps coming in above it.

Note that market cap can be used just like share price to create valuation ratios. Just as you can divide share price by earnings per share to create a P/E ratio, you can divide market value by the aggregate earnings amount (not the per share amount) to create the same thing.

Enterprise Value

Similar to market cap, but with two important adjustments. Enterprise value starts with market cap, then adds the company's debt and subtracts its cash. It shows the amount it would cost you to buy a company in its entirety and pay off everything it owes while pocketing any available cash. For that reason, enterprise value is particularly useful for takeover analysis.

Dividend Rate

The per-share amount a company pays in dividends each year. Companies often change their dividend rates, so there are a couple of ways to come up with an annual number. One is to use the sum of dividends a company has paid over the last year. Another is to assume it will keep making payments the same size as its most recent one. (That's sometimes called indicated dividend yield.) Some stock screeners offer both choices. Dividend rate isn't much use without comparing it to a company's share price, so you'll likely use dividend yield more often.

Dividend Yield

A stock's dividend rate divided by its share price is the yield. Dividends not only provide investors with income, they show that a company's managers understand the importance of returning profits to shareholders. Also, because dividend yields increase as share prices fall, searching for healthy dividend yields is like searching for modestly priced stocks. Perhaps for that reason, dividend yields have long been a predictor of share price gains. See the New Dogs screen in Chapter 16 for a way to boost the predictive power of dividends and find great stocks.

Dividend yield is a welcome add-on for many stock screens, but be careful not to get too greedy for yield. For example, don't look for stocks that yield at least 5 percent, or more than three times the broad market's average yield at present, simply because you've determined that you need to pull a 5 percent income off your portfolio. Some companies carry high yields only because their share prices have tumbled due to significant problems. Those problems might lead them to cut their dividend payments. Better to look for dividends of, say, 1 percent or greater, but also look for signs that bode well for future stock gains, such as rapid earnings growth. If you need to generate a 5 percent income with your portfolio, consider adding bonds or other income investments rather than hunting for oversized dividend yields. Better yet, use the best income investment going: a portfolio of great stocks combined with the occasional sell order.

Payout Percentage

Payout percentage is the amount a company spends on dividends divided by its earnings over the same period. It is most often used to make sure companies aren't paying out too much of their earnings as dividends, the idea being that a temporary dip in earnings might force them to cut their dividend payments. Stocks often tumble when their dividend payments are cut, so it's important to make sure the companies you invest in can afford their dividends. One common strategy is to combine a demand for healthy dividend yields with another for, say, payout ratios below 75 percent.

If you're following a dividend-based strategy, you might want to make sure payout percentages aren't too low, either. Consider a 2003 study in *Financial Analysts Journal* written by a pair of well-known money managers, Robert Arnott and Clifford Asness. The latter likes to give his research papers punchy titles, like "Stock Options and the Lying Liars Who Don't Want to Expense Them." This one was called "Surprise! Higher Dividends = Higher Earnings Growth." One of the presumptions about companies with high payout ratios is that their growth has slowed. They no longer need to fund expansion projects, so they might as well pay out nearly all of their earnings as dividends. Arnott and Asness showed that's not necessarily the case. Looking at stock data since 1946, they found that companies in the top 25 percent of the S&P 500 in terms of payout ratios produced real earnings growth (that's earnings growth minus the rate of inflation) of 4.2 percent a year on average. Companies in the lowest 25 percent saw real profits shrink by 0.4 percent a year.

Arnott and Asness came up with two possible explanations for the finding. One is that since companies hate to cut their dividends, high payout ratios signal a high level of confidence in future earnings growth. The other is that high payout ratios help prevent *empire building*. That's the well-documented tendency of companies that hoard cash to end up blowing it on ill-advised acquisitions that expand management's influence, but not the stock's price.

Profitable Companies

Profitability clues are an important indication of a company's pricing power and cost efficiency. Most are margins that measure the percentage of profits remaining after subtracting a certain set of expenses from sales.

Companies in different industries produce vastly different levels of profitability, so don't screen for margins that are above a particular number. Rather, make comparisons to industry averages. Also, keep in mind that you're looking for the best stocks, and not necessarily the best companies. It does little good to search for the most profitable companies in each industry if shares of all of those companies are expensive.

Better to look for companies with growing margins. Those signal that operational improvements are afoot. Sometimes those improvements roll out gradually over several quarters or years, and sometimes analysts and investors are slow to fully appreciate the pace of improvement.

Also, margins can grow because of cost-cutting, but cost-cutting can only carry a company so far. By looking for growing sales and improving margins, you're more likely to find companies that are collecting higher prices because their products are in greater demand.

Gross Margin

Gross income divided by sales equals gross margin. This can be a quarterly figure, or an annual figure of a multiyear average. Gross income, recall, is the profit a company clears after paying its manufacturing costs. An increase in gross margin might mean that a company has reduced its labor costs or its raw material costs. Its labor costs might be falling due to outsourcing or to shifting foreign production to a cheaper country—from Germany to Brazil, for example. If raw materials costs are falling, it's often because of an external change in commodity prices.

Operating Margin

Operating income divided by sales is the operating margin. This is the percentage of sales left after subtracting for both manufacturing costs and corporate costs for things like salespeople, advertising, and headquarters operations. Operating costs are often easier to reduce than manufacturing costs, simply because they tend to be more plentiful. Plush extras are more likely to find their way into the offices of people making the decisions than onto the factory floors of people cutting the steel.

Higher margins are generally better, but when hedge funds and takeover specialists shop for companies to buy, they sometimes look for below-par operating margins. They know that those companies might trade cheaply today because their earnings are being eaten up by corporate costs, and that new management can slash those costs and resell the company at a higher price.

Net Margin

Net income divided by sales. This is the percentage of a company's sales left as profits after subtracting for everything—manufacturing costs, operating costs, research costs—and making any final accounting adjustments. Net margin is perhaps not as useful as gross and operating margin for sizing up a company's profitability because those extraordinary charges and credits that go into calculating net income can produce wide swings in the measure. A company that writes down assets one quarter due to damage from a freak storm might see its net margin plunge, even though it's improving its profitability on an operating level.

SGA/Sales

The percentage of operating costs a company pays as a percentage of its sales. It's related to operating margin but with two key differences. First, companies try to reduce this measure, not increase it. Second, unlike operating margin, which takes out for both operating and manufacturing expenses, SGA/sales uses only operating expenses to give investors a better idea of which companies are saving or wasting money on the corporate level.

There are other measures of profitability. Any measure of profits divided by sales is a profit margin, so you might see terms like EBITDA margin, pretax net margin, and so on.

Growing Companies

Just about any company you invest in should be growing its sales and earnings. It might be growing slowly but have shares that are cheap enough to make a purchase of them worth your while. It might be growing quickly enough to make its seemingly expensive shares a relative bargain. It might be suffering a dip in earnings this year but might also look set to resume its growth next year. Whatever the case, there should be reason to believe the company will do more business in the future than it's doing today. So you'll use these measures often in your screens.

We can't actually tell how fast a company is growing right now. Not right at this moment, anyhow. We can do two things. We can see what analysts have to say about how quickly the company will grow its sales and earnings over the next couple of years. Since such forecasts are more a measure of perception than reality, I'll look at them shortly in the section on company popularity. We can also see how quickly a company has grown its sales and earnings in recent years on the assumption its future pace of growth will resemble its past one.

Be aware of a couple of things. First, earnings growth without sales growth is a sign of cost-cutting and while that's laudable, it can only last for so long. Better to look for companies that are growing their sales, too. Second, the life cycle of companies is such that growth rates tend to slow as they age. One of two things tends to happen. Either companies lose out to competitors, or they succeed so well that they saturate their markets and have trouble finding new customers as fast as they once did. Microsoft, for example, increased its sales by an average of 38 percent a year during the five years ended 1996 and by 23 percent a year during the five years after that. In early 2007 Wall Street projections put the company's sales growth at 14 percent and 11 percent over its next two fiscal years. What went wrong? Nothing. Things went so right, though, that nearly everyone who uses a computer at home or work uses at least one Microsoft product. The company's sales base is now so big that it's unrealistic to assume it will return to the growth rates of its youth.

Slowing growth isn't necessarily a bad thing, so long as growth rates are slowing in a controlled fashion rather than plummeting. Just make sure you get more than you pay for. A company whose growth is slowing should have cheap shares. If you're buying fast-growth stocks with high price/earnings ratios, make sure those growth rates aren't likely to plunge in coming years. Also, search from time to time for companies with accelerating sales growth. That's often a sign something is going unusually right. It might be that a new product has suddenly caught on or that an advertising campaign is working. Sales accelerations can roll out gradually over several quarters and catch other investors by surprise. Just make sure a sudden quickening in a company's sales isn't merely the result of it buying another company.

Keep one other thing in mind when screening for a company's sales and earnings growth in its most recent quarter. There are two period comparisons you can use: sequential growth and year-over-year growth. *Sequential growth* is a quarter's percentage increase versus the most recent quarter—the amount sales increased from the second to the third quarter, for example. *Year-over-year growth* measures the percentage increase versus the same quarter a year ago—third-quarter sales this year compared with third-quarter sales last year. The latter is usually better. Some companies operate in seasonal industries. Toy stores, for example, book the bulk of their sales in the Christmas quarter. So it wouldn't make sense to compare their Christmas quarter with their fall quarter. Sequential growth is generally most useful when you're screening for the young companies with blazing growth rates. A start-up whose sales will likely double this year, for example, is ramping its income up fast enough that the difference between its second and third quarters might more than offset seasonal differences between those quarters. Unless otherwise stated, all quarterly growth rates in this book refer to year-over-year growth.

Sales Growth

The best stock screeners will let you search for sales growth over the past quarter (sequential and year-over-year), past calendar year, and most recent fiscal year, and give you a three-year average and a five-year average. They will also allow you to screen for sales growth relative to industry, index, and database averages.

How you use sales growth depends in part on which type of screen you're running. If you're searching for value stocks, it's unrealistic to think they'll be attached to companies with rapid and accelerating sales growth. Better to look for companies with merely healthy sales growth of say, 10 percent to 15 percent a year in recent years. If you're searching for growth stocks, you'll likely want sales growth rates of more than 20 percent a year. You'll also want to make sure sales growth isn't slowing too sharply, and maybe that it's even accelerating. If you do, start with a healthy three-year figure—say, 20 percent. Then screen for one-year growth that's faster than three-year growth and quarterly growth that's faster still. When researching your screen survivors, weed out companies whose sales acceleration is due only to acquisitions.

Earnings Growth

If you're searching for companies whose income growth has recently accelerated, you're better off using sales than earnings. That's because sales are less susceptible to quarterly dips and bumps due to one-time accounting charges. That said, one without the other does a company little long-term good. Sales growth without earnings growth is a sign of aggressive discounting. By lowering prices, companies can ring the register as much as they like, but doing so won't increase their profits and might even cut into them. Earnings growth without sales growth, meanwhile, might mean a company is cutting its manufacturing or operating costs or is easing up on research spending. Cutting wasteful spending is fine, but companies that are having trouble growing their sales sometimes cut operating costs too aggressively just to hit this quarter's earnings target. That can produce ugly results next quarter and beyond.

It's best to look for earnings and sales growth of comparable amounts to make sure companies are bringing in more business and are doing so responsibly. Use a measure of earnings that excludes extraordinary charges if you can, so that you're gauging just the effect of current operations.

One exception: If you're searching for fast-growing start-ups that aren't yet profitable, you'll have to rely on sales growth alone before profits turn positive. Since you can't look for earnings growth, make sure that sales are at least ramping up faster than operating costs and that the company isn't blowing too much money on big investments.

Just like with margins, there are other measures of income that you can use to gauge growth: operating income, EBITDA, and so on.

Well-Managed Companies

Stock-screeners can't tell you where a company's boss went to school, how many hours a week he works, or whether he weighs in on every issue or merely picks good department heads and lets them handle things. But those are merely cosmetic items, anyway. Results matter more, and stock screeners are great at looking for those.

Well-managed companies earn big returns on their resources, and they do so efficiently. If a company has a machine that makes ring-shaped breakfast cereal, a good manager might introduce two new flavors of that cereal that can be made with the same machine. That increases sales without requiring much by way of new investments. Also, that same manager might make sure that the company is moving cereal quickly from the production line to customers, and collecting quickly for sales that are made on credit.

Notice that many of the measures that follow use an ingredient from the income statement and another from the balance sheet, whereas the profitability and growth measures used only income statement ingredients. That's because ideal managers can generate big profits using a minimum of stuff. The income statement measures the profits. The balance sheet measures the stuff.

Return on Equity

Return on equity (ROE) is earnings divided by shareholders' equity. Shareholders' equity, also called net worth, is a company's total assets minus its total liabilities. ROE essentially shows the amount of profit a company squeezes out of the money shareholders entrust to it. That makes it one of the most useful financial measures you'll screen with.

Some investors confuse the return in return on equity with stock returns. The two are different, but an impressive ROE can lead to plentiful stock returns. Think of ROE as a company's internal returns. It's the profit the company generates with the money you've provided it with as a shareholder. All things equal, if one company can produce a 25 percent internal return on your money and another manages only a 10 percent return, the first company is more likely than not to attract new stock buyers and see its stock price rise over time. Another way to think of ROE is as something of an upper limit on a company's earnings growth. A company with a 25 percent ROE would be expected to increase the earnings it reports by no more than 25 percent each year.

ROE is made up of three ratios multiplied together: earnings/sales (or profit margin), sales/assets (or asset turns), and assets/equity (or leverage). Recall from your fraction multiplication days in school that when you put the three side by side, the two sales cancel each other out, as do the two assets. That leaves earnings/equity, which is return on equity.

If a company's ROE is weak, the problem lays in one or more of the three component ratios. Perhaps prices are too low or costs are too high, as in the case of the deli owner mentioned in Chapter 1 who stuffs a $5 sandwich with $6 worth of pastrami. That's a *margin problem*. Maybe a company is tying up too much in assets to produce too little in sales; consider a pizza shop owner who invests in a high-volume oven but does only a modest slice business at lunchtime. That's an *asset turns problem*. (It's also a sign that every analogy I come up with relates to food.) Managers seeking to improve their company's ROE—and many are paid according to how well they do just that—can address either of these two areas.

They can also increase the third ratio, leverage, by increasing debt faster than equity. Therein lays one of ROE's weaknesses, useful as it is. Some changes that have little to do with a company's operations can give its ROE a big boost. For example, by writing down nonperforming assets, a company records a charge on its income statement for a single year, reducing its earnings that year. But it reduces its equity permanently. So after the first year its earnings will be back to normal and its ROE will have increased. Also, keep in mind that ROE says nothing about how much debt a company has. Companies that rely more on borrowing than on issuing shares in order to raise capital tend to have higher ROEs. So it's a good idea to screen for debt levels whenever you screen for ROE.

Return on Assets

Return on assets (ROA) equals earnings divided by assets. Unlike ROE, this measure doesn't take into consideration a company's financing decisions, and so doesn't end up rewarding companies for relying too heavily on debt.

Just like ROE, ROA may be thought of as being made up of component ratios multiplied together. In fact, it's made up of the first two ratios that ROE is made of. That's earnings/sales (profit margin) and sales/assets (asset turns). Multiply the two together and the two sales cancel out, leaving earnings/assets, or ROA. Note that the ratio we've left out is leverage. ROA isn't concerned with whether a company's assets are paid for by taking on debt or by issuing shares. It just focuses on how much earnings those assets are producing.

ROA has a weakness, too. (It actually shares this weakness with ROE.) It tends to flatter a company that relies more on intangible assets like ideas than on fixed assets like plants and equipment. That's because the value of intangible assets that a company develops on its own rather than purchases generally doesn't show up on the company's balance sheet, and therefore doesn't make its way to the bottom side of the ROA ratio.

Return on Invested Capital

Return on invested capital (ROIC) is, well, a bit complicated. I've seen more than a dozen ways to calculate the measure. Which calculation is best depends on which type of company you're looking at. For that reason, it's often not included in stock-screening software. It attempts to include on the bottom side of the ratio only those items that represent resources management has available to it to invest, like common and preferred equity and long-term debt.

All three of these measures—ROE, ROA, and ROIC—are useful. Don't buy shares of a company before you've looked at the internal return it is generating on its resources. I've included one of these measures in only some of the screen strategies, so be sure to build one of them into your postscreen research process. Also, note that returns on anything will only be as accurate as the measure of returns being used. Good stock screeners will include a glossary of their variables that will tell you how they're constructed. If a screener uses GAAP earnings with no adjustments, be aware that one-time charges and credits can skew its return ratios. In that case, you might be better off building a return ratio yourself using a measure of earnings that excludes extraordinary charges.

Receivables Ratio

The receivables ratio is sales divided by receivables. This gives an idea of how efficiently a company is extending credit to its customers.

Receivables amount to the value of goods that customers have received but haven't yet paid for. By extending credit, companies make it easier for their customers to place routine orders. A company's receivables ratio should be in line with those of its industry peers. A rising ratio could mean customers aren't paying.

Inventory Turnover

Sales divided by inventory equals inventory turnover. This shows how quickly a company is moving merchandise through its warehouses and onto customer shelves. If you use this measure, make comparisons to industry averages. Too low of an inventory turnover might mean unsold merchandise is building up, which can lead to clearance pricing and reduced profits. Too high of an inventory turnover could mean the company is having trouble producing enough to meet demand.

Asset Turnover

Sales divided by assets equals asset turnover. This is one of the component measures of ROE, recall. A high asset turnover means a company is generating heaps of sales using little by way of plants and equipment. An online store would be expected to have a higher rate of asset turnover than a walk-in store, because it doesn't have physical stores as assets. Note that high profit margins—a second component measure of ROE—can make up for modest asset turnover, and then some. In the case of the walk-in store, it might be able to charge higher prices than the online store because of its ambiance and overall customer experience. Low-margin companies should have high asset turnover to make up for those margins.

Financially Strong Companies

Strong companies generate plenty of cash to meet their financial obligations. Debt is related to financial strength, but what matters more is a company's ability to make payments on its debt. We'll look first at some measures of debt and then at some measures of how affordable that debt is.

Debt/Equity

Debt divided by equity shows how much a company has borrowed relative to its net worth. A ratio of 1.0 indicates a company has borrowed an amount equal to its net worth. Don't read too far into that, though. The worth of a company is determined by its ability to generate profits for you, and not solely by the value of hard assets recorded on its balance sheet. What matters more than the level of a company's debt is the amount of interest it pays for that debt relative to the profits it generates using the debt. Also, different industries have different levels of acceptable debt. If you wish to remove companies with high debt levels when running stock screens, use industry comparisons to do so. Note that debt for purposes of the debt/equity ratio might refer to long-term debt or it might refer to total liabilities. The best screeners offer a choice of the two.

Debt/Capital

Debt divided by the sum of equity and debt is really a restatement of debt/equity. If a company's total capital is a pie with two slices, debt and equity, then debt/equity is the ratio of one slice to the other and debt/capital is the ratio of one slice to the entire pie. Use it in the same manner you'd use debt/equity.

Debt Service Coverage Ratio

This is earnings divided by debt service. Debt service is the principal and interest a company must pay on its debt over a given period. Often, the measure of earnings used for this calculation ignores one-time accounting charges and credits. A debt service coverage ratio of 1.0 means a company is making only enough money to make its debt payments. The higher the number, the better.

Interest Coverage Ratio

This is EBIT divided by interest expense. Recall that EBIT stands for earnings before interest and taxes. This measure is similar to debt service coverage ratio, but doesn't consider principal payments.

Current Ratio

Current assets divided by current liabilities is a measure of a company's ability to pay its short-term obligations using its readily accessible resources. This measure might be overrated as a gauge of financial strength. It says nothing about how easily those current assets on the top of the ratio can be converted into cash to pay for those current liabilities on the bottom side of the ratio. A company with a warehouse full of out-of-style sweaters might have a high current ratio thanks to its inventory, but might stand little chance of selling that inventory quickly.

Quick Ratio

Current assets minus inventories, divided by current liabilities is a safer measure of solvency than the current ratio because it ignores inventories, which may or may not be useful in meeting short-term obligations. But it still includes receivables as part of short-term assets. That's a gamble, too. What happens if a company is having trouble collecting from its customers? Its quick ratio might be high despite the company's lack of ability to pay its bills.

Cash Ratio

Cash and cash equivalents, divided by current liabilities, is the most conservative of the measures of short-term financial liquidity, because it measures a company's ability to meet its obligations without relying on inventories and receivables.

Cheap Companies

The practice of determining what companies and their shares are worth is called *valuation*. There are two broad ways to go about it, only one of which lends itself neatly to stock screening. The first way, suitable only for company-by-company research and not for stock screening, is to figure out how much a company will make over a future time period—say, over the next 10 years—and to then put a price on that amount today. Analysts often do that with projected cash flows. It used to be popular to do that with projected dividends.

The act of coming up with a current price for future income is called *discounting*. Think of it like this: How much would you pay me today for the right to receive a dollar five years from now? I hope you didn't say a dollar. You should get a discount to compensate you for tying up your money for that long. How much of a discount you should receive depends in part on the risk that I won't make good on the dollar I'm supposed to give you five years from now.

When you hear the term *discounted cash flow analysis*, that means that an analyst is projecting how much cash a company will produce over some future time period, and then figuring out how much you should pay for that cash today based on the company's risk.

Discounted cash flow valuations are more about human judgment than math and are too complicated for stock screeners. So you'll search for cheap stocks using less comprehensive measures, but ones that are also less subject to human error. You'll use what's called *comparative valuation*.

Comparative valuation refers to judging whether a company is cheap or expensive relative to other companies in the same business. That's done using the ratio of its stock price to a measure of either how much money the company makes or how much wealth it has amassed.

Price/Sales

For this ratio, share price is divided by sales per share, often from the past 12 months. This might be the most useful valuation measure you'll find. The price/earnings ratio is more popular, but price/sales is more closely correlated with stock gains. Read why in Chapter 21 on the Sales on Sale screen.

Price/Earnings

The price/earnings ratio, or P/E, is share price divided by earnings per share. If you're already familiar with just one stock clue, this is probably it. P/E can be measured with trailing 12-month earnings or forecasted earnings for the next calendar or fiscal year. Also, you can use any of several measures of earnings. If you're screening for forward-looking P/E ratios, they're usually based on forecasts that exclude one-time accounting charges and credits. If you're screening for past earnings, you might want to select a measure that excludes such extraordinary items.

I'm not sure how good your chances are of finding bargain stocks by looking for P/E ratios alone. The measure is so popular that everyone searches for low P/Es. That may be one of the reasons the predictive power of low P/E ratios seems superior to that of low P/Es in research. If you do screen for low P/Es, it's far better to make comparisons within industries rather than looking for ratios below a certain numerical cutoff. In other words, look for companies whose P/Es are in the bottom 25 percent for their industries rather than those whose P/Es are below, say, 15.

Sometimes you'll see P/Es compared with their own historical values. Someone will say a stock is cheap because its P/E is 12 and that's below the stock's five-year average P/E of 15. You can use some screeners to search for P/Es that are below their historical values. I don't recommend it. Companies just aren't that stagnant. There's no reason a company should fetch the same P/E today that it did five years ago if things about the company have changed since then.

PEG Ratio

The PEG ratio is the price/earnings ratio divided by the earnings growth forecast. For example, a company with a P/E of 12 that's expected to grow its earnings by an average of 10 percent over the next five years has a PEG ratio of 1.2.

Sometimes past P/Es are used to calculate the PEG ratio and sometimes projected ones for the current fiscal year are used. Also, the growth forecasts might be for the next year, next three years, or next five years. There's no right way to do it, as long as you use the same method for each company you look at. Stock screeners will take care of that for you.

The PEG makes little sense mathematically. For one thing, it divides a ratio by a percentage without first converting one to the other; your grade school arithmetic teacher would frown on such a tactic. But I find it far more useful than the P/E ratio. The PEG ratio is the only valuation measure in this section that works for comparisons between companies in dissimilar industries. That's because it normalizes those P/E ratios for the growth rates each industry is capable of producing. So feel free to compare, say, a cement maker to an e-commerce outfit using the PEG ratio, and feel free to screen for PEGs below, say, 1.5 rather than below industry averages.

Keep in mind that the PEG ratio is only as useful as its underlying projections are accurate. So use it for a rough gauge of valuation, not as a precision tool.

Price/Free-Cash-Flow

This is share price divided by free cash flow per share. What makes this measure useful is that it's a gauge of both valuation and financial strength. Free cash flow is the real, excess cash that companies generate each quarter that can be used to pay dividends, reduce debt, and repurchase shares. Companies that produce plenty of free cash are financially stable. Companies that produce plenty of free cash relative to their share prices might be cheap.

EV/EBITDA

This ratio is simpler than it looks. EV is *enterprise value*. Recall that it's equal to a company's market value (the total cost of all its outstanding shares) plus its debt, minus its cash. Recall also that *EBITDA* stands for earnings before interest, taxes, depreciation, and amortization. It's a measure of a company's underlying earnings potential that ignores certain charges related to past investments. You can think of EV/EBITDA as the takeover-price/money-being-made-right-now ratio.

Note that you can stick EV on top of any valuation ratio you can stick price on top of. I won't go through EV/sales and EV/earnings, but you might see them.

Price/Book Value

This ratio is share price divided by book value per share. Book value is the amount you would receive if you liquidated a company today. Because companies today tend to use more intellectual capital and less physical capital than companies in the past, you might think P/B is a somewhat outdated measure. In fact, it's the basis of one of the most powerful strategies in this book, the Combination Platter screen detailed in Chapter 22.

Popular Companies

Popular companies are ones that attract plenty of stock investors and for whom analysts issue optimistic estimates and recommendations. Some measures of popularity are better than others at predicting higher share prices.

Price Change

One of the most useful clues you'll encounter is a stock's recent price change. Stocks that are on their way up are more likely than not to keep climbing, particularly when you look for them in the right way. See how to do that in Chapter 12, which covers the Buy High, Sell Higher screen.

Most screeners will allow you to search for stocks that are up a certain amount over the past week, quarter, six months, or year. Some will allow you to search for price changes relative to an index such as the S&P 500 index, so you can search for stocks that are outperforming the broad market. Share price gains are often the first outward sign that something is going right for a company.

Insider Buying/Ownership

The term *insiders* refers to a company's executives, board members, and so-called *beneficial owners*—those with more than a 10 percent stake. Studies show that insiders tend to outperform the broad market when purchasing their own shares. Since such transactions must be publicly reported almost immediately, you can search for companies with big insider buying anytime you like by using a stock screener. See the Follow the Leaders strategy in Chapter 19 for tips on how to spot the most prescient insider buys.

You're better off screening for companies with large dollar amounts of insider buying rather than large numbers of shares bought, since the latter will tend to produce companies with low share prices. You can search for insider selling, too, but it doesn't have the same predictive power as buying. Again, see Chapter 19 for why.

Insider ownership levels don't have the same predictive ability as insider buying, but I like to look for at least a smidgen of insider ownership when I screen for small, fast-growing companies. I view it as a disincentive for managers to issue too many shares in order to raise capital, since issuing shares would dilute the value of their stock holdings.

Institutional Buying / Ownership

Institutional buying isn't as good a sign as insider buying, since insiders tend to produce better returns than, say, mutual funds. But institutional ownership means some deep-pocketed investors have an interest in your stock. Ownership levels that aren't too high (say, greater than 5 percent but below 50 percent) mean that those same investors have plenty of shares left to purchase should they wish to.

Change in Short Interest

Short interest is the number of shares of a company that have been sold short. *Short selling* refers to selling borrowed shares of a company in hopes the price will drop, allowing the short seller to buy them back on the cheap and pocket the difference. A little short selling is usually meaningless. High levels of short selling could be cause for concern; you should check to see why so many investors are betting against the stock.

Extremely high levels of short selling could be, ironically, a positive sign. That's because those shares must eventually be bought back. If the stock rises instead of falls, short sellers develop paper losses. Since short sales must be made in margin accounts and backed up with collateral in the form of cash or investments, mounting paper losses might lead the short seller to have to deposit more collateral. Eventually, the short seller might be pressured into buying back the stock at a loss. If enough short sellers do that at the same time, a condition called a *short squeeze* can develop. You've heard of panic selling? Think of a short squeeze as panic buying. It can be plenty profitable for those who own the stock at the time.

It's possible to search for stocks with short-squeeze potential. I haven't included a short-squeeze screen in the strategies section of this book, because I view it as more of a short-term tactic than a long-term investment strategy, and because opposing short sellers carries more risk, I think, than simply searching for great stocks. If you want to search for short-squeeze candidates, though, look for four things. The first is a large recent percentage increase in short interest. The second is a high short interest ratio (discussed next). The third is a bit of institutional ownership. That puts investors with deep resources on your side of the trade. The fourth is reason to believe short sellers are wrong. That means you should look for modest stock valuations and potential for growth, things you would look for in most other screens.

Short Interest Ratio

The short interest ratio is the ratio of a stock's short interest to the number of shares it trades on an average day. Think of this as the slingshot in the aforementioned short-squeeze search. The more shorted shares there are to be bought back relative to average trading volume, the higher the stock should climb during a squeeze. Again, focus on the long-term stock-picking strategies laid out in this book rather than hunting for squeeze candidates. The payoff is bigger and the risk is lower.

Average Analyst Recommendation/Change in Recommendation

These are those buy, sell, and hold recommendations you hear about. As mentioned earlier, studies show that stocks with heaps of buy recommendations don't necessarily do better than stocks without them. Changes in these recommendations are a better predictor of stock gains. See the Rising Expectations screen in Chapter 18 for more.

Average recommendations are useful for your value screens. Value stocks should have plenty of popularity left to gain and little to lose, so eliminate stocks with average recommendations of buy and strong buy from your results.

Analyst Forecasts

You can screen for *forward* valuation measures that are built with forecasted sales and earnings rather than past sales and earnings if you like. Estimates are usually available for the current, not-yet-complete fiscal year and the next one. You can also screen for this year's and next year's growth rates based on those estimates. Finally, you can often screen for long-term EPS growth rate. That's the annual rate at which analysts figure a company's earnings per share will grow over the next five years or so.

There's a trade-off involved whenever you use growth estimates instead of or in addition to past growth rates. You gain time but lose reliability. That is, you get a more current picture of a company's prospects, but there's a good chance that picture is a bit off. The further out the estimates go, the less reliable they are. If you're using a forward P/E based on the current fiscal year's forecast and the company has already booked earnings for its first three quarters, you're using a pretty reliable measure. Long-term EPS growth rates, meanwhile, amount to little more than educated guessing. That's why I include analyst estimates in the section on popularity rather than in the ones on growth rates or valuation.

Use forecast-based data, by all means, but use it judiciously and be skeptical of predictions for astounding growth rates five years into the future. I tend to doubt any projection that calls for five-year earnings growth of greater than 30 percent, since that's getting close to Microsoft-in-its-heyday growth. Also, watch out for long-term EPS growth forecasts that are higher than this year's growth forecasts. How can a company be expected to grow earnings by 25 percent a year over the next five years if it's only expected to grow them by 12 percent this year and 10 percent next year?

Note that PEG ratios are based in part on long-term EPS growth rate projections. That's why the PEG is only a rough gauge of valuation. If a company's PEG ratio seems suspiciously low, make sure the long-term EPS growth projection is reasonable.

Part Three

STRATEGIES

Chapter 11

How to Use the Strategies

The purpose of the screen strategies that follow is to generate short research lists, and not automatic buy lists.

Given two groups of stocks, one that will produce average returns of 10 percent a year over the next several years and another that will produce annual returns of 13 percent to 18 percent, you stand a better chance of selecting winning stocks from the second group. As we look at each strategy, we'll review ample evidence that suggests it can produce average returns significantly higher than the broad market's returns.

Also, given two groups of stocks, one with 8,000 of them and another with 12, you'll be better able to perform research on the second group. Any stock screen can reduce the field of candidates to a manageable number. The ones that follow can reduce the number of candidates while at the same time improving their average returns.

There are more than a dozen strategies covered, which raises the question of whether you should choose one and stick with it or run a few of them from time to time in search of your next great stock. Before we come to the matter of faithfulness, let's see how the two broad approaches to stock picking compare.

Growth Screens versus Value Screens

Stock market pros love to argue this one—whether it's better to invest in growth or value stocks. I've never quite understood the labels. How can an investor choose between growth and value? Surely we should only invest in companies that are likely to grow, so growth investing sounds like a good idea. But there's no point in buying a stock unless you think its price will be well higher in the future than it is today. That makes today's price something of a value. So maybe value investing is the better bet.

Really, there's little point in choosing between the two approaches. The labels are imprecise and the definitions are sloppy. Just about all investors take into consideration a company's growth prospects and its stock valuation before deciding whether to buy shares. You should, too.

Investors looking to compare the past performance of growth and value stocks must first come up with a methodical way to tell the two apart. Most often, they rely on one of two clues: a valuation ratio like the price/earnings ratio and the rate of past or predicted earnings growth.

Some investors consider low-P/E stocks to be value stocks and high-P/E ones to be growth stocks. If that's the definition, clearly value stocks are better. Stocks with low P/E ratios outperform those with high P/E ratios over long time periods. Some investors call a stock with fast earnings growth a *growth stock* and one with modest earnings growth a *value stock*. If we use this definition, we should buy only growth stocks. There's a clear link between earnings growth and share price gains over long time periods.

Often investors consider both valuations and growth rates when labeling stocks. They use something similar to the PEG ratio discussed in Chapter 10. Recall that it divides a stock's P/E ratio by its earnings growth rate. In doing so, it puts growth and value stocks on equal footing. A stock with a P/E of 12 and an earnings growth rate of 8 percent has the same PEG ratio of 1.5 as a company with a P/E of 30 and an earnings growth rate of 20 percent.

Viewed that way, growth stocks don't exist in one basket and value stocks in another. Rather, stocks with the best mix of growth and value characteristics exist on a spectrum. You can buy stocks from one end of that spectrum (low P/Es, low growth rates) or the other (high P/Es, high growth rates).

In common practice, the difference between growth and value stocks isn't as severe as in the previous example. Consider the Russell 3000 style indexes, one for growth stocks and one for value stocks. The company's Web site, Russell.com, explains how they're constructed: "Based on ongoing empirical research of investment manager behavior, the methodology used to determine growth probability approximates the aggregate broad market growth manager's opportunity set."

I have no idea what that means. Better to define the two indexes by what's inside them. Companies in the Russell 3000 Growth index at the time of this writing carry an average P/E ratio of 20.8 and are projected to grow their earnings by 19.9 percent a year over the next five years. For the Russell 3000 Value index, the average P/E falls to 14.8 and the average earnings growth forecast is 17 percent. If we divide those P/E ratios by the earnings growth rates for each index, we get a PEG ratio of about 1.0 for the growth index and 0.9 for the growth portfolio. The indexes are pretty close in terms of what you get relative to what you pay for, but with a different mix of attributes.

Which does better over long time periods? The Russell indexes haven't been around long enough to get a good read on the numbers, but other studies suggest growth and value are equal. In *Common Sense on Mutual Funds,* author John Bogle, founder of the Vanguard family of funds, looked at the performance of growth and value stocks over the 60-year period ended 1997. He found that growth stocks retuned an average of 11.7 percent a year and value stocks 11.5 percent. That's a small enough difference to call the matter a tie.

You've no doubt seen studies that suggest one style vastly outperforms the other. One of two things is probably skewing the results. The methodology might be off. That is, the growth stocks might be "growthier" than the value stocks are cheap, or vice versa. More likely, though, the time period under study is too short.

Over short time periods the returns for growth stocks and value stocks are often sharply different. That has more to do with investor sentiment than the inherent worth of growth of value stocks. For that reason I think the terms *popular* and *unpopular* more accurately characterize the difference between the two stock-picking styles.

Investors are willing to pay up for popular stocks because they're excited about the earnings growth of those companies. They're not willing to pay as much for value stocks because those companies are growing their earnings a bit slower. When the stock market is rising, investors are more confident about future earnings, so they're willing to pay higher prices for stocks with forecasts for plenty of earnings growth. When the market is falling or flat, investors are less interested in forecasts than they are in getting a good deal relative to earnings that a company is producing today. Over long time periods—say, 50 years or more—the two classes of stocks perform similarly. But most of us don't have 50 years to invest. That's why we can't just treat growth and value stocks as the same thing.

In Bogle's study, growth stocks were clear winners during the first three decades, then value stocks shined for nearly the next decade, then growth stocks, then value stocks again. Since that time the lead has switched a couple more times. Growth stocks soared in the late 1990s when investors chased technology shares. Value stocks have outperformed since the popping of the Internet-stock bubble in the middle of 2000.

If you know whether the next year or two is going to bring a bull market or a bear one, you'll know whether to load up on growth or value stocks. I haven't found a reliable way to forecast that, though. I just know that it tends to go up nicely over long time periods. Better to buy a mix of growth and value stocks.

Faithfulness Is Overrated

Market strategists often say the best thing a stock picker can do is decide on a strategy and stick with it. I'm not convinced that's true.

Let's look at the New Dogs strategy we'll cover in Chapter 16 as an example. It's a regimented and easy-to-follow strategy. If you're familiar with the Dogs of the Dow strategy, you know it starts with the 30 stocks that make up the Dow Jones Industrial Average and selects the 10 with the highest dividend yields at the start of each year. The New Dogs strategy makes an adjustment for the fact that companies are increasingly choosing to return cash to shareholders through share repurchases in addition to dividends. I'll save the details for later, but suffice it to say the strategy still selects 10 stocks each year. Like the original Dogs strategy, it tends to select stocks whose share prices have fallen because yields increase as prices fall. It's a value strategy.

The performance numbers that support the strategy are great—better than those for the original Dogs strategy. I'm convinced that if you use the strategy to pick 10 stocks each year, and you do so for two or three decades, you'll handily outperform the broad stock market. But there are two problems with putting that into practice with all your money. First, you might not have the discipline to follow such a strategy. You wouldn't be nearly alone. Most great stock-picking strategies underperform the market some years. It's not easy to stick with a strategy when it doesn't seem to be working. The second and bigger problem is that we've just seen that value stocks can underperform or outperform growth stocks over periods of longer than a decade. If you follow the New Dogs strategy exclusively, you'll own all value stocks.

Follow any of the strategies you like in any way you like. Use them in a regimented way where you buy 10 or so of the screen survivors based on some ranking. Or, use the screens to narrow the field to likely winners so that you can pick the one or two you like most. Either way, you'll have significantly improved your chances of finding great stocks. Just be sure that the great stocks you end up with have a mix of qualities. Some should be popular and some should be unpopular. You should have big companies and small ones, domestic companies and foreign ones, and a mix of different industries.

Read up on asset allocation elsewhere to figure out a mix of stocks that's right for you. Then be as faithful or unfaithful in your stock-screening strategies as you please, as long as you end up with a good blend of company attributes.

Feel Free to Tinker

I've laid out specific lists of clues, or recipes, to use when putting together each screen. These aren't rigid instructions. Feel free to adjust the numbers to produce longer or shorter lists of stocks, as long as the broad theme of the screen remains intact.

Chapter 12

The Buy High, Sell Higher Screen

I magine that you've stumbled upon the perfect growth stock. It's a chain of casual restaurants that's doing big business in your area: Cha-Ching Bar & Grill. The menu offers burgers and ribs and such that draw hearty eaters, but also healthy dishes that appeal to calorie counters. In just a couple of years of operation, Cha-Ching has become the place to go to watch the big game, to stop in for a drink after work, to eat before going to the movies, and to host a kid's birthday party.

Not only are the restaurants packed for lunch and dinner on most days, but also management has figured out other ways of making money. Cha-Ching does a brisk delivery and pick-up business. It sells its popular barbecue sauce by the bottle, along with Cha-Ching shirts and baseball caps. Gift certificates have also proven a hit.

You decide to check out the company on the Internet and are delighted to find that it's publicly traded. That is, you can buy shares.

Looking through Cha-Ching's financials, you learn that sales and earnings are growing nicely and margins are gradually improving as the company expands. Debt is negligible. Comparable dining chains, you notice, have several hundred restaurants, are spread across broad swaths of the country, and are still growing. Cha-Ching has just 25 restaurants, but has plans to open 8 more this year. It just opened its first restaurant in a neighboring state.

You're thrilled with the discovery. You just happen to live near and eat at a restaurant in the early stages of what could blossom into a nationwide expansion and years of big stock gains. There's just one problem. Cha-Ching might be small and fairly local, but apparently it's not exactly a secret among investors. Its share price has more than doubled over the past year and now stands at an all-time high.

You decide to hold off for the moment. A stock that's gone up that quickly can come down just as fast, and you don't want to be the last one who buys it before it falls. If only you had gotten in sooner. For now, you'll just watch the stock. If the share price tumbles in the future, perhaps you'll reconsider a purchase. After all, buy low and sell high—isn't that what they say?

Remember that sentiment. It's part of the reason why, more likely than not, Cha-Ching's shares are headed higher.

A stock's price contains information about whether that stock is likely to do well in the future. Okay, the price alone doesn't tell you much. If the only thing you know about a stock is that it trades at $18 a share, you can only guess as to whether it's worth buying. But if you add just two more pieces of information to that price, you end up with one of the most powerful predictors of future stock gains. One of those pieces of information is the percentage by which the share price has risen or fallen in recent months. The other is how far the share price is from its 52-week high.

All things equal, stocks that have gained nicely over the past six months to a year tend to outperform the broad stock market over the next six months to a year. Stocks that are up nicely and are sitting near their 52-week high prices are overwhelmingly more likely to beat the market, and for a longer time.

That might sound simplistic. After all, if picking good stocks was just a matter of checking whether they're up big in recent months, stocks would go up forever and making money on them would be easy. Momentum traders in the late 1990s practiced just that sort of folly in chasing technology shares to absurd highs.

Granted, price momentum alone isn't reason enough to buy a stock. Also, day traders sometimes use price momentum blindly without regard to stock valuations. But neither changes the fact that price momentum as a predictor of stock gains works, and works well.

Researchers have studied the predictive power of price momentum since at least the 1960s. Early results were confusing. Studies showed the past winners were indeed more likely than not to outperform the broad market. But at the same time other studies showed that contrarian strategies worked, too. That is, past losers also tended to outperform the market. Both, of course, can't be true.

In 1993, a pair of UCLA finance professors, Narasimhan Jegadeesh and Sheridan Titman, published a landmark paper in the *Journal of Finance* titled "Returns to Buying Winners and Selling Losers: Implications for Stock Market Efficiency." It shed some light on earlier studies. Looking at stock returns between 1965 in 1989, the pair found that stocks that had outperformed the broad market over the past 3 to 12 months tended to continue outperforming it by a margin of a few percentage points per year. But they only maintained that lead for the next 3 to 12 months. After that, the stocks were more likely to do just the opposite—to underperform the broad market.

That's enough of a finding to make money from if you're nimble. Several stock picking services, including ones offered by Value Line and Investors Business Daily, have compiled winning records by looking, in part, for *relative strength,* or a stock's past performance relative to a broad market index. But for individual investors looking to pick winning stocks, there's a better way.

In a 2004 study titled "The 52-Week High and Momentum Investing," also published in the *Journal of Finance*, Thomas George of the University of Houston and Chuan-Yang Hwang of Hong Kong University of Science and Technology set out to crack the code of price momentum. Rather than look for stocks that had merely posted big gains in recent months, as Jegadeesh and Titman had done, they looked for those that were within 5 percent of their 52-week highs. The two approaches might sound similar, but there's a critical difference. A stock that has soared over the past year but has dipped in recent weeks might turn up on a search for big gainers, but not on a search for stocks that are near their highs right now. The 52-week-high method serves to identify stocks with more immediate price momentum.

George and Hwang looked at stock prices between 1963 and 2001. They studied the performance of a *long/short portfolio*—one that buys stocks within 5 percent of their 52-week highs while selling short stocks that are within 5 percent of their lows. They compared the results with a long/short portfolio that used the old method, buying past gainers and selling short past losers without regard to 52-week high and low prices. The gainers/losers portfolio beat the broad market by a pace of 4.5 percentage points a year, but held that pace for only about six months after each portfolio rebalancing. After that, the returns started to disappear. The 52-week high/low portfolio beat the broad market by 7.8 percentage points a year. Remarkably, the returns stayed strong for more than five years.

The implications for investors are powerful and specific. Price momentum matters. The direction that a stock has moved in recent months is more likely than not the direction it will move in coming months. That's particularly true of stocks that are making new 52-week highs.

That's not to say that investors should buy stocks simply because they're going up. The aforementioned studies looked at thousands of stocks and reported average results. Plenty of individual stocks within the samples contradicted those results. The fact that shares of Cha-Ching Bar & Grill have soared over the past year isn't, on its own, reason enough to buy the stock. Investors should still look into the financial strength of the company and whether those shares are expensive relative to the money the company is making now or the money it will likely make in the future. But the evidence shows that an investor shouldn't disregard the company simply because its stock is at an all-time high. In fact, investors should seek out such stocks for further research.

George and Hwang offered a theory in their paper as to why stocks hitting new highs tend to move even higher. "Traders appear to use the 52-week high as a reference point against which they evaluate the potential impact of news," they wrote in the study's concluding remarks. "When good news has pushed a stock's price near or to a new 52-week high, traders are reluctant to bid the price of the stock higher even if the information warrants it. The information eventually prevails and the price moves up, resulting in a continuation."

That sounds a bit like *anchoring*, which we discussed in Chapter 3. Investors who decide not to buy shares of Cha-Ching simply because of its rapid price increase over the past year are not behaving entirely rationally. They're not assessing the stock on its merits—the company's profit growth and so on. Rather, they have decided that they don't want to buy a stock at the highest price it's ever fetched. They are anchored in the former range in which the stock traded, and are uncomfortable with the new one.

But new high prices are a normal occurrence. If stocks moved in a straight-line progression rather than erratically, they'd hit new highs every day. An investor who shies away from a stock hitting new highs does so because he views it as expensive. Ironically, with so many investors thinking the same thing, stocks hitting new highs are often kept less expensive than their growth prospects warrant. That's why you should screen for them.

Almost any stock screener offers investors a way to screen for stocks that are up big in recent weeks or months. Many also allow for a search for stocks that are within a certain distance of their 52-week-high prices. Run such a search as often as you like. Unlike screens based on quarterly financial data, a screen based on price momentum will produce results that change day to day. And a rising share price is often the first visible sign of good news for a company. Investors who watch a stock closely sometimes bid its share price up on the anticipation of operational improvements. Only later will those improvements turn up in screens that look at earnings, sales, and cash flow.

Of course, you'll want to do your best to avoid stocks that are soaring because of frenzied speculation, Internet chat rooms, and the like. So keep price momentum surges to companies of a decent size (say, sales of $100 million a year or more) and also screen out thinly traded companies (those with average daily trading volume of less than 100,000 or so shares). Remember that the goal in using a price momentum screen isn't simply to chase high fliers. It's to create an early warning system for stocks that are on the move. You should research the screen results carefully in an effort to determine why shares are rising and whether company fundamentals suggest they have further to run.

Buy High, Sell Higher Screen Recipe

- Share price within 5 percent of 52-week high
- Sales greater than $100 million
- Average daily trading volume greater than 100,000 shares

Reduce the field of survivors further if you like by looking for attributes of fast-growing companies, such as big recent increases in sales. Also, you might add a requirement that company insiders own at least 5 percent of shares. That makes management less likely to raise money by issuing shares too freely, something young companies are prone to do.

- One-year sales growth greater than 20 percent
- Insider ownership greater than 5 percent

Chapter 13

The Impatient Value Screen

Value investing is said to favor the patient. Find a company whose true worth is unrecognized by Wall Street, tuck some of its shares away, forget about them for a long time, and eventually the market will come around. Unfortunately, waiting on an unloved stock isn't as easy as it sounds. Feelings of doubt crop up, particularly as you watch other stocks do well while the one you've adopted just sits there. Sometimes the relationship becomes a begrudging one. You've already held the stock for three years now and, by golly, you're sticking with it until it makes some money.

Patience is overrated. Sure, it feels good when that stock you've stuck with for years suddenly starts to rally. But it doesn't feel nearly as good as when the same thing happens to a stock you've held for just a few weeks.

There might be a way to search for bargain stocks to hold for the next five years while adding some potential for them to pay off over the next five months. I call it the Impatient Value screen. It combines a traditional value search with a smidgen of price momentum.

Those two might sound contradictory. Value stocks, after all, are ones whose share prices have been beaten down to the point where they look attractive relative to measures of income (sales, earnings) or company worth (book value). Price momentum suggests just the opposite: a popular company whose share price is being bid higher.

In fact, the goal of any value investor isn't just to find underappreciated stocks. It's to find underappreciated stocks that will eventually win more popularity and higher share prices. In other words, the goal is to find value stocks that will eventually become price momentum stocks.

Combining the two attributes, then, isn't contradictory at all. A traditional value search looks for underpriced stocks that are due for a recovery. An Impatient Value search looks for underpriced stocks whose recovery has already begun. There's a trade-off involved, but it's a pretty attractive one. The stocks that turn up on an impatient value screen won't be sitting at the lowest prices they've seen in recent months. But if the findings on price momentum covered in the previous chapter hold, the stocks will be more likely than traditional value stocks to head higher in coming months.

The American Association of Individual Investors, whose stock screener we looked at in Chapter 8, tracks its own value/price-momentum screen, which it calls a *Value on the Move* screen. The results have been impressive. Since 1998 the AAII says the portfolio value has increased more than eightfold. It's unrealistic to expect it to continue producing results like that. Those returns are based partly on back testing for the period between 1998 and 2003, when the association began publishing the results of the screen on its Web site. But in 2004, 2005, and 2006, the screen returned a healthy 54.1 percent, 23.1 percent, and 18.3 percent, beating the broad market each year.

The screen looks for PEG ratios below 1.0 but above 0.2. Recall that a stock's PEG ratio is its price/earnings ratio divided by the rate at which its earnings are projected to grow over the next several years. So a stock with a P/E ratio of 12 that's projected by analysts to grow its earnings at 10 percent a year over the next five years has a PEG ratio of 1.2. The broad stock market at the time of this writing has a PEG ratio of about 1.5, so the AAII screen looks for stocks that appear cheaper than the market by at least a third relative to their earnings growth outlook. The lower a stock's PEG ratio, the better, but PEGs that are too low should be cause for suspicion. They're likely the result of either a data error or a financial result that doesn't reflect the company's true performance, such as a one-time surge in earnings on a lawsuit settlement that makes a stock's P/E ratio look temporarily depressed. Thus, the screen sets a lower PEG ratio cutoff of 0.2.

The AAII screen makes other demands for things like recent earnings growth and strong share price gains. Based on the price momentum findings from Chapter 12, I prefer to replace the demand for gains with one that looks for stocks within 5 percent of their 52-week highs.

Expect such a screen to turn up two types of stocks. The first is one that has been struggling for a long time but has recently started to recover. The second is one that has been rising steadily over the past year but still looks inexpensive relative to the company's growth prospects. Either type of stock is worth a closer look.

Impatient Value Screen Recipe

- PEG ratio below 1.5
- PEG ratio above 0.2
- Share price within 5 percent of 52-week high
- Trailing 12-month sales greater than $100 million
- Average daily trading volume greater than 100,000 shares

If you'd like to reduce the field further, either lower the PEG ratio ceiling to 1.0 or add a demand for a recent increase in a company's earnings estimates, such as next-year EPS estimate raised within past four weeks. This is another sign that the company might be turning things around.

Chapter 14

The Surprise, Surprise Screen

I f you want to feel slow, try this: Watch a financial news channel and wait for a company to report much-better-than-expected earnings. Then, as fast as you can, call your stockbroker or log on to your trading account. Try to buy the stock before it moves higher. Make sure you use a limit order—one that specifies the maximum price you want to pay. Chances are, though, you won't bother placing the order. By the time you pull up a quote on the stock, it will already be up considerably from where it was before the news broke.

It used to be possible to make a living by trading off of earnings news. I witnessed the death of the practice in the 1990s while working as a stockbroker. My best customer and the company's biggest commission generator had two things that allowed him to get to trades faster than other investors. The first was a Cold-War-style hotline—a dedicated phone on my desk that rang the moment he picked up the handset in his rural, upstate New York home. The second was something largely unknown to individual investors at the time: real-time, scrolling financial headlines delivered over a computer monitor. The service was wildly expensive, but for "Flip," as I'll call him, it was well worth it.

I kept Flip happy by answering his calls on half a ring and placing his trades within seconds. Sometimes he'd call a minute before the headline was due and just wait on the phone with me in order to save the half a ring. In a typical trade, Flip would be in and out of several thousand shares within five minutes. He made great money a half point at a time, and I racked up discounted but plentiful commissions for my company. (I was lucky to have those commissions, because, as I mentioned in Chapter 4, I was the worst mutual fund salesperson in the business.)

The Internet put Flip out of business. It took away his two biggest advantages. First, it gave anyone with an active-trader brokerage account from the likes of E*Trade and Ameritrade the ability to view real-time quotes and scrolling headlines. Second, it gave investors access to someone who can enter their trades even faster than me and my dedicated hotline: themselves. In the early days, when great earnings news would come out on a $35 a share company, Flip would likely buy at $35.25 or $35.50. Once everyone and their barber started day trading on the Internet, that same stock would hit $37 before Flip had a chance to get in. At first he started chasing stocks higher, but that proved less profitable. Soon he began trading less frequently. Finally, Flip settled into something that for him would have been unheard of just a few years prior: long-term investing.

Neither Flip nor I knew it at the time, but there's another way to turn good earnings news into winning stock purchases. It doesn't require constant attention to a scrolling news service. It doesn't require fast access to a trading screen. In fact, the strategy is perfect for slowpokes and long-term investors. Best of all, it's perhaps more lucrative than Flip's frantic method.

For about 40 years, researchers have documented an odd phenomenon they call *post-earnings announcement drift*, or PEAD. In a perfectly efficient market, stocks would price in all available news nearly immediately. So when a company reports quarterly earnings that top Wall Street's forecast, we'd expect to see its shares jump right away, and then fall back into a fairly predictable pattern of returns. But that's not what happens. Stocks tend to jump immediately, but they also tend to drift gradually higher for up to a year, outperforming the broad market in the process.

PEAD isn't exactly a secret among professional investors. Earnings-momentum mutual funds are based on the phenomenon. The existence of PEAD was first reported by accounting professors Raymond Ball and Philip Brown in an award-winning paper in 1968 titled, "An Empirical Evaluation of Accounting Income Numbers." Since then, more than a thousand studies have been published on the subject. You'd think investors would have caught on, and would pounce on stocks with positive earnings surprises to the point where they no longer go on to produce market-beating returns in later months. But they don't; research published within the past couple of years shows PEAD-based strategies still outperform the broad stock market. The fact that PEAD has predicted generous stock returns for more than four decades has done much to dispel the notion that markets are, after all, perfectly efficient.

That said, the returns aren't what they used to be. That makes sense. Earnings surprises today are smaller than they used to be. More analysts contribute to consensus estimates. More data are available for them to use in developing their forecasts. Companies have learned how to hint about their performance so as to avoid disappointment after earnings announcements. A PEAD-based strategy can still beat the market, but only by a few percentage points a year, judging by recent research. But you can add a twist to the strategy that new research suggests will help you clobber the market.

Some upside earnings surprises represent fantastic news. Others are nothing to get excited about. The difference has to do with more than just the size of the surprise. It has to do with the quality of the surprise. When Apple first made a mockery of Wall Street's earnings estimates by selling far more of its iPod music players than analysts anticipated, that was great news for investors. But when a struggling carmaker beats estimates by closing plants, laying off workers, and cutting production in order to slash costs, it's not exactly reason to celebrate.

The difference between surplus earnings that come from a booming business and those that come from accounting tweaks and cost cuts shows up clearly on companies' income statements. A company that's prospering because its products and services are selling well reports not only impressive earnings but impressive sales, too. One that's struggling to find new customers but is nonetheless working to doll up its earnings will report languishing sales. Simply put, upside earnings surprises are far more interesting to investors when they're accompanied by upside sales surprises.

A few years ago, that idea occurred to Narasimhan Jegadeesh, a finance professor at Emory University. Jegadeesh has more than just an academic interest in such matters. In the past, he has sold stock-picking models to Morgan Stanley and Deephaven Capital Management, a hedge fund. Jegadeesh and a partner, Joshua Livnat of New York University, looked at thousands of earnings announcements between 1987 and 2003. They ranked the announcements according to the percentage by which they had beaten or fallen short of analyst estimates. They simulated buying each stock the day after its announcement and holding for six months.

In a 2006 paper titled "Revenue Surprises and Stock Returns," published in the *Financial Analysts Journal*, Jegadeesh and Livnat detailed a fascinating finding. The top 20 percent of stocks in terms of upside earnings surprises outperformed the broader market by three percentage points over six months. The top 20 percent in terms of sales surprises outperformed by 2.6 percentage points. But a cross sample of the two—shares of companies that handily surpassed both earnings and sales estimates—trounced the broad market's return by 5.3 percentage points over the six-month period, or by more than 10 percent if you annualize the figure.

You'll have a difficult time mimicking the study in your own portfolio, unless you run an institutional trading desk that can make hundreds of transactions each quarter. But the implications for individual investors are clear. It pays to take an interest in companies that beat earnings estimates and those that beat sales estimates. It can be especially lucrative to seek out companies that have recently beaten both.

There's another advantage to adding a sales demand to a search for earnings momentum. Sales are listed at the top of companies' quarterly income statements. Earnings are listed at the bottom. Between the two, manufacturing and corporate costs are deducted, taxes are paid, adjustments for depreciation and one-time items like lawsuit settlements and asset sales are made, and more. Corporate accountants, in other words, do most of their fiddling below the line on which sales are reported. It's not impossible to embellish sales results, but it's far more common for companies to tinker with earnings. So if you're someone who doesn't quite trust all companies to get their numbers exactly right each quarter, sales can provide an added measure of reliability.

Most stock-screening tools will let you search for upside earnings surprises over the past quarter or past year. A few also let you search for upside sales surprises. To stay true to the study methodology, simply search for stocks that have beaten earnings and sales estimates in their most recent quarter by a wide margin—say, 10 percent or more. Also, you might want to screen for something called *standard deviation of estimates*. A low one means that analysts are tightly clustered in their earnings forecasts. In other words, they more or less agree on how much a company should earn, making surplus earnings all the more surprising.

Surprise, Surprise Screen Recipe

- Past-quarter upside earnings surprise greater than 5 percent
- Past-quarter upside earnings surprise above industry average
- Past-quarter sales surprise greater than 5 percent
- Past-quarter sales surprise above industry average
- Standard deviation of estimates below industry average
- Trailing 12-month sales greater than $100 million
- Average daily trading volume greater than 100,000 shares

Make sure those earnings surprises aren't large merely because they're coming off of a small base. A company that was projected to earn a penny last quarter and earned two cents produced a huge percentage surprise, but not a big one in dollar terms.

To reduce your field of screen survivors further, look for things like strong recent sales growth and modest price/earnings ratios:

- One-year sales growth greater than 15 percent
- Forward price/earnings ratio below industry median

Chapter 15

The Tomorrow's Breakthrough Screen

Most of us have seen what happens when a largely ignored company announces a breakthrough drug or a sudden advance in computer chips. Its shares usually soar right away. Wall Street scrambles to figure out just how much in profits the new technology will add over the next several years. Those who owned the shares before the announcement are left with an enviable choice: Sell them at a big profit or hold out for what might be an even bigger one.

Of course, for every one of those people who hold the right company at the right time, there are scores who sit on shares of technology companies that never produce the big breakthroughs. Wouldn't it be nice if there were a way to predict which companies are due for lucrative discoveries, and buy their shares while they're still cheap?

I'm glad I asked. As it turns out, there is a way to identify companies that are due to cash in on new developments. It doesn't require tea leaves or tarot cards. The only mysticism involved is that of America's accounting standards.

Technology breakthroughs are born of two parents. The first is an idea. The second is money. Ideas are difficult to predict and almost impossible for investors to learn about soon enough. But money is easy to follow. Before a new, say, memory chip goes into production, it goes through years of mock-ups, prototypes, tests, remakes, and so on. Technology companies spend piles of money each year to support such research. Because companies have become good at channeling research spending into projects that are most likely to pan out, the spending translates into future profits in a fairly predictable fashion. The spending is reported for accounting purposes long before the breakthroughs are announced. Follow the spending, then, and you follow the future profits.

It gets better. Because of the way research and development spending is treated for accounting purposes, it makes current earnings look lousy. That means that at precisely the moment a company is investing to build a future profit stream, its shares look unattractive. Buy shares of such companies at their least flattering moment and hold on until the fruit of all that research spending starts rolling in, and you can secure big profits. More on how to do that in a moment.

At the heart of America's accounting standard is something called the *matching principle*. It states that, when possible, costs should be paired with the sales they produce for purposes of financial reporting. For example, suppose it costs a company $2 to manufacture a toy car that it then sells for $10. It manufactures a million of the cars for a cost of $2 million but only sells a thousand for $10,000 this quarter. Rather than deduct the huge manufacturing expense from the puny sales this quarter, the company deducts $2,000—just the portion related to the cars it actually sold. This figure is labeled *cost of goods sold* on the company's income statement.

Sometimes companies make huge upfront payments for things like new plants and equipment that are meant to produce sales, not just over the next few quarters, but for many years to come. These payments qualify for special treatment as capital investments. They don't have to be deducted from sales. For purposes of calculating current profits, it's as if the company never spent the money. Of course, the cost of capital investments will be deducted from earnings eventually. It gets broken down into smaller quarterly charges that are deducted over the projected useful life of the new plant or equipment. That process is called *depreciation*.

It's easy to envision why the matching principle is important. Suppose companies subtracted the entire cost of new factories from their earnings as soon as the payments were made. A chipmaker would post a huge loss in the quarter it built a factory. In the following year, revenues from the new chips would roll in and the company would post enormous profits. Someone looking through several years of the company's financial results would see chaos—wild swings from staggering losses to record profits and back again. A lender wouldn't know whether to lend. An investor wouldn't know whether to invest.

So the matching principle is useful, but it's not perfect. For one thing, it makes a mess of research and development spending.

If you think about it, R&D seems like just the kind of thing that should be treated as one of those capital investments that can be deducted little by little from sales. It's a big upfront payment that produces sales, not just this quarter or even this year, but starting a few years from now and lasting perhaps a decade or more. According to the matching principle, we should break down R&D spending into small quarterly charges to be deducted gradually over many years. But there's a problem with doing that.

For companies, capital investments are much more attractive than expenses. Expenses, remember, reduce earnings right away. Capital investments leave earnings intact. If you're a manager whose bonus is paid according to this year's earnings and you have a choice of whether to treat a particular payment as an expense or a capital investment, you have a strong incentive to choose capital investment.

The thing about R&D spending is that it's not as clear-cut as the cost of a new piece of equipment such as an aluminum smelter. Companies have to buy far more than protective goggles, lab coats, and beakers to conduct research. Some of the things they buy, in fact, don't look like research. A new computer, for example, might be used for a couple of months in the lab and then be sent to the ad sales department.

Companies figured out long ago that they can stuff all kinds of expenses into their research and development budgets, thereby qualifying for preferable accounting treatment. So the government changed the rules. Since tracking the use of each item companies buy would be impossible, all research and development spending must now be treated as an ordinary expense.

That's right. Money that's used to create new sources of profits for shareholders is treated no differently from money that's blown on the company Christmas party. All of it serves to shrink earnings right away. That's good news for you. Anything that serves to hide the appeal of good stocks from other investors creates a buying opportunity for those who are in the know.

Not all companies spend big on research and development. Banks and retailers have little to develop. Drug makers and technology companies, by contrast, are largely research-driven. In all, roughly one in five publicly traded companies spends at least 10 percent of its sales on research.

One way to find bargains among all those companies is to use something called the *price/R&D ratio*. It works much like the price/earnings ratio. On the top of the ratio is the company's share price. On the bottom is the money it has spent over the past year on research and development.

A low P/R&D ratio tells a story about a company. Its share price is most likely beaten down. Management, presumably, is under pressure from shareholders to get the stock moving. Companies faced with that challenge typically look for ways to slash costs, thereby improving earnings. But a company with a low P/R&D ratio is, at least in part, doing just the opposite. It's continuing to plow dollars into research, an expense that reduces current earnings. Just when management is under the most pressure to maximize earnings, it's choosing to spend on something that reduces them. That means one of two things. Either management is foolish, or it's spending on something of significant importance.

The latter is more likely to be the case. A 2001 University of Illinois study titled, "The Stock Market Valuation of Research and Development Expenditures" looked closely at the link between research and development spending and operational improvements. The study tracked more than 1,800 instances during the 50 years ended 2001 when companies that already spent sizable amounts on R&D started spending substantially more. On average, over the five years following the spending increases, profit margins for those companies increased one to three percentage points faster than profit margins for peers. Stock returns beat the broad market by about five percentage points a year.

A 2004 Georgetown University study titled "An Examination of Long-Term Abnormal Stock Returns and Operating Performance Following R&D Increases" discovered something similar with low P/R&D ratios. It looked at research spending and share prices for all U.S. companies over the 20 years ended 1995. Shares of companies with low P/R&D ratios, it found, outperformed the broad market by about six percentage points a year.

Put it all together and you have the makings of a powerful stock screen. Note, though, that it's not enough to merely look for high levels of R&D spending. Studies have failed to find a link between a company's level of spending and its future stock performance. As long as a company spends a steady amount each year on research, it seems, its profits are fairly predictable and its shares have usually already priced those profits in. The combination of low P/R&D ratios and recent increases in R&D spending, though, tends to produce fat profits for both companies and their investors.

To build an R&D screen you'll need a stock screener that offers R&D as one of its data points and that has a formula builder. You'll find R&D grouped under income statement data, since it's treated as an ordinary expense. Start with decent-sized companies—those with sales of at least a few hundred million dollars a year. Make sure your companies spend at least 5 percent of their sales and 5 percent of their assets on research. Then look for low P/R&D ratios and recent increases in research spending. To create your P/R&D ratio, divide market value by trailing 12-month R&D spending.

Tomorrow's Breakthroughs Screen Recipe

- Trailing 12-month R&D spending at least 5 percent of sales
- Trailing 12-month R&D spending at least 5 percent of assets
- Trailing 12-month R&D spending greater than prior 12-month R&D spending
- Price/R&D ratio below 20

Note that I've used a numerical cutoff for the P/R&D ratio instead of an industry comparison. None of the stock screeners covered in this book allow users to make industry comparisons on measures they build themselves using formula builders. I've started with a fairly generous P/R&D ratio of 20. If you wish to further reduce your list of screen survivors, gradually reduce the ratio to 15 or so.

To reduce the list further, look for respectable sales growth in recent years and modest price/earnings ratios:

- Three-year sales growth greater than 12 percent
- Forward P/E below industry median

Chapter 16

The New Dogs Screen

I can't tell my *loukoumades* from my *glykismata* or my *amygdalopita* from my *diples,* but I love a good Greek dessert. I was thrilled a year ago when a Greek pastry shop opened just a few blocks from my New York City apartment. One of the owners ran the store with the help of his daughters. The other, I learned, was a passive investor, or was meant to be, at least. I sampled some of the honey-drenched unpronounceables. They were tasty, so I kept going back. So did a lot of my neighbors. Within several weeks, the shop had lines at the counter nearly every night.

Then it closed, with no explanation. Curious, I asked a couple friends who own restaurants in the area what had happened. (Small business owners secretly delight in making their best it's-a-pity face and explaining why a new competitor failed.) They told me that the two owners couldn't agree on how to split the profits. Their argument had become bitter, with both threatening to close the business down. Finally, they both did.

Profit squabbles have long been a challenge for shared companies. Early merchant shippers had a way to avoid the problem. I mentioned it in Chapter 4. After each voyage, they'd simply dissolve and distribute the profits to investors. The emergence of perpetual share-issuing companies like Dutch East India—companies that issued stock for longer than a single voyage—was made possible by a financial innovation. This innovation helped smooth relations between those waiting quietly to receive their share of a company's profits and those managing the company. In an era when accounting standards were few, it was better than promises or trust. It was cash in the pocket—a *dividend*.

Dividends prove two important things about a company. First, they show that it's making money. Companies can sometimes get creative in their financial reporting to make things look better (for investors) or worse (for the tax man) than they actually are. But companies are unlikely to continue making quarterly cash payments to shareholders if they're not, in fact, generating quarterly cash. Second, dividends show that a company's managers understand the importance of returning profits to shareholders.

Perhaps that's why throughout the history of stocks big dividends have been reliable predictors of share price gains. Through 1635, Dutch East India paid dividends only occasionally, but from then on it paid one every year. These weren't the 1 percent-a-year dividends today's investors might be used to. Dutch East dividend payments sometimes topped 60 percent a year. The bigger the dividends grew, the more attractive the shares became. By 1650, they had multiplied sixfold in value.

If big dividends generally lead to higher share prices, finding stock bargains should be easy. Simply look for companies with the lowest share prices relative to their dividend payments. In other words, look for the highest dividend yields.

One of the most popular investment strategies of the 1990s, and one that still has plenty of fans today, does just that. It's called the *Dogs of the Dow* strategy. Start with the 30 companies that make up the Dow Jones Industrial Average. They are all giants with household names like Caterpillar, Coca-Cola, and Microsoft. Choose ten of these companies that have the highest dividend yields. Buy them. Wait a year. Repeat.

The strategy was popularized by Michael O'Higgins in his 1991 book *Beating the Dow*. Wall Street soon whipped up investment products based on the strategy: Dogs of the Dow trusts, Dogs of the Dow mutual funds, Dogs of the Dow managed accounts, and so on. Demand for them was intense. Not only was the strategy simple, which made for an easy sales pitch, but the back-tested performance numbers were impressive. Over the 50 years ended 1995, the Dogs beat the Dow by three percentage points a year.

Investors who bought packaged Dogs of the Dow investments in 1995 might be growing impatient. Despite an impressive showing in 2006, the strategy over the 11 years since 1995 has produced annual gains of 6.7 percent and dividends of 3.4 percent, no match for the Dow's 9.4 percent yearly gains and 2.1 percent dividends. The once-unstoppable Dogs have been making puddles in investors' portfolios.

Have dividends lost their appeal? And if so, should the Dogs strategy be retired?

No, dividends haven't lost their appeal. They've just lost some of their predictive power. And don't ditch the Dogs just yet. With a tweak to the strategy, they might have their best years ahead of them.

The link between dividends and stock gains started to weaken in the 1980s just as companies began to change the way they return profits to shareholders. If you run a company that generates more cash than it needs to fund growth projects, make acquisitions, and pay down debt, and you decide (wisely) not to horde cash on your balance sheet, you have two main choices as to how to spend the money on shareholders. You can pay dividends or you can repurchase shares.

When companies buy back their shares, they increase their earnings per share, since it's now calculated using a lower share count. That tends to make the remaining shares more valuable. Theoretically, dividends and share repurchases should work out to be an equal deal for investors. They end up with either cash in their pockets or more expensive shares in their accounts. But one external element gives share repurchases an edge in terms of efficiency: taxes.

For most of the twentieth century (before which there was no regular income tax in the United States), dividends were taxed as ordinary income. Some investors argue this is unfair because it represents double taxation. The money is taxed once to companies as profits and again to shareholders as dividends. A 2003 compromise between politicians who wanted to repeal the dividend tax and others who wanted to leave it alone resulted in a lower rate. Rather than be taxed as ordinary income, dividends are at the time of this writing taxed at a maximum rate of 15 percent. Still, they're taxed. Money spent on share repurchases escapes double taxation.

Since share repurchases put more money to work for investors than dividends, they represent the better deal. So you'd think they would have eclipsed dividends in popularity shortly after the start of the income tax. But until 25 years ago, most companies didn't buy back stock. There were a few instances of companies using share repurchases to manipulate their stock prices. They quietly bought shares to generate enthusiasm among investors, who soon followed with buy orders of their own. Once the share price had ballooned, the companies would issue new stock at higher prices. Respectable companies avoided repurchases, partly for fear of looking like manipulators.

Rule 10b-18 sought to end the abuse. Enacted by the Securities and Exchange Commission in 1982, it spelled out for companies a series of requirements that must be met when they buy back stock. These include restrictions on volume and timing. The rule produced an unexpected boom in repurchase activity. By following its guidelines, companies could repurchase all the shares they liked with impunity, as long as they weren't buying based on important information that hadn't yet been disclosed to the public.

Before rule 10b-18, share repurchases made up only around 10 percent of total spending on shareholders, and dividends, the rest. Today, spending on repurchases and dividends are about equal.

This got a group of four finance professors thinking about dividend yields, and whether they're as meaningful today as they were a few decades ago. Dividend yields, after all, are a gauge of just one of the ways that companies spend on shareholders. If repurchases and dividends are similarly beneficial for investors, wouldn't it be better to define yield as total money spent on shareholders, whether spent on shares or paid out as dividends? Back when repurchase spending was just a trickle, the question might not have mattered much. But now that repurchase spending has matched dividend spending, we might need to change the way we think about high-yield stocks.

Jacob Boudoukh, Roni Michaely, Matthew Richardson, and Michael Roberts at Arison (Israel), Cornell, New York University, and Wharton, respectively, developed a measure they call *net payout yield* and described it in a 2004 paper titled "On the Importance of Measuring Payout Yield: Implications for Empirical Asset Pricing." To calculate the measure, add the dollar amount a company spent on dividends over the past year to the amount it spent on repurchases. Subtract the amount it collected from new share issuances. Divide the resulting figure by the company's market value. The four studied returns for thousands of companies for 32 years ended 2003. The broad stock market during that time returned a handsome 13 percent a year. Stocks with high dividend yields did even better, returning a couple of extra percentage points per year. Those with high net payout yields, though, beat the broad market by a whopping five percentage points a year. In dollar terms, the broad market would have turned a $10,000 investment during their study period into a half million dollars. Stocks with high net payout yields would have turned it into more than $2 million.

Next the four professors turned their attention to the Dogs of the Dow. They looked at performance figures between mid-1983, when repurchase activity started to pick up, and the end of 2005. The Dogs returned 16.2 percent a year during that period, beating the Dow Jones industrial average by nearly three percentage points a year. But an updated set of Dogs based on net payout yield rather than dividend yield returned an astounding 19.1 percent a year.

Investors can use this information to build a variety of stock screens. They can follow a modified version of the Dogs strategy. They can search for the highest-yielding stocks in a broader index like the S&P 500. Or they can simply replace dividend yield with net payout yield in a growth and income search—one that looks for companies with impressive profit growth and meaty yields.

I'll focus on the first one, a modified version of the Dogs strategy. Running the search is slightly more complicated than just looking for big dividends. Dividend yields are displayed prominently on most financial Web sites and are built in to just about all stock screening tools. Not so, net payout yield. You have to build the measure yourself. That means you need a screener that lets you build your own formulas.

The money companies spend on dividends and share repurchases and the money they receive from new share issuances are all listed on their cash flow statements. Calculating net payout yield, then, should be as easy as adding the past four quarters' worth of dividend payments to share repurchases over the same period, subtracting share issuances, and dividing the resulting figure by market value.

There's just one problem. Cash flow statements are usually reported cumulatively. That means that third-quarter figures, for example, are usually the sum of figures from the first, second, and third quarters. So you can't just add up the past four quarters of dividends and repurchase activity; you'll end up with numbers that are far too high.

I'll give you two solutions, one that's easy but not as timely and another that's timely but also a pain in the can. Try the difficult one first. If you get stuck, use the other one.

1. *Pain-in-the-can method:* Start with the 30 Dow Jones Industrial Average stocks. Have your screener display amounts for dividend spending, share repurchases, and share issuances for each of the past five quarters. Export the results to Excel. Now eyeball each company's numbers. They should snowball up until each company's fourth quarter and then drop to a lower number for its first quarter of the following year. You should be able to tell which quarter the most recent figure is from, and work out the math in a new column to get a trailing 12-month figure. For example, if the most recent figure is from a company's third quarter, add that figure (which is actually the sum of quarters one, two, and three from this year) to the difference between the company's fourth and third quarters from the prior year (which is actually just its fourth quarter amount). You'll have to do this company-by-company, because not all companies operate on the same fiscal year. The whole process should take you 15 or 20 minutes once you get the hang of it.

2. *Easy method:* Just use figures from companies' most recent fiscal years, rather than the trailing 12-month period. The figures could be more than half a year old, but most of the Dow industrials operate on fiscal years that match the calendar year and report their full-year results by March. So if you run the screen each April, you'll get fresh figures for most of the companies.

I won't bother listing a screen recipe for this one because it would contain only one clue (index = Dow Jones Industrial Average). Most of the work is done using the data your screener can provide in the report.

Who knows? Maybe data providers will make things easier by crafting those figures into a net payout yield that companies can include in their screeners and financial Web sites can list next to dividend yield.

Chapter 17

The Bold Is Beautiful Screen

"I can't believe what a POS that thing is," wrote one Wall Street analyst in an e-mail in December 2000. "POS" stands for point of sale in the retail business, but the analyst wasn't writing about retail. He was writing about an Internet marketing stock, and his "POS" stood for "piece of sh*t." The assessment was an accurate one. The company, Lifeminders, has since dissolved for lack of profits. Its former shareholders lost all of the money they invested.

The analyst, Henry Blodgett of Merrill Lynch, might've won praise from investors for his tough but honest warning. The problem is, he didn't send this message to investors. He sent it to a colleague at his firm, while at the same time publishing research reports recommending the rest of us "accumulate" shares. This wasn't an isolated incident. Six months prior, he had called Excite@Home, a now defunct Internet portal, "such a piece of crap!" in an internal e-mail, while publishing "buy" recommendations on the stock.

Analysts have a vested interest in making accurate recommendations. Why would one of them praise a stock in public and bash it in private? Blame the conflict of interest facing analysts who work for firms that also provide investment banking services to companies.

Investment banking services include helping companies issue new shares to investors in order to raise money. The fees for such services are significant. A company seeking to issue new shares would naturally prefer to do business with the firms that can help create demand for the shares among investors. Firms that have large retail brokerage businesses with plenty of account holders can do just that. Their analysts can even publish reports recommending that those account holders buy shares of the company paying for investment banking services. Of course, it's unethical for an analyst to recommend a stock just to please one of his firm's customers. There should be a strict divide between the research and investment banking departments of Wall Street firms. But in the madness of the late 1990s technology stock boom, some analysts forgot, bent, or broke the rules.

New York's Attorney General at the time, Eliot Spitzer, sued Merrill Lynch over what he claimed was a conflict of interest, bringing to light the aforementioned e-mails in the process. Merrill Lynch settled for $100 million. Blodgett was charged in 2003 by the Securities and Exchange Commission with securities fraud. He settled without admitting any wrongdoing and agreed to a lifetime ban from the securities business.

The Blodgett case and similar ones have since tarnished the reputation of analysts and the firms they work for. Many investors believe Wall Street's buy, hold, and sell recommendations can't be trusted and that analyst reports should be ignored and replaced with one's own research. They're right about the first part, but wrong, I think, about the second. Buy recommendations shouldn't be trusted, not because they're dishonest but because they're wrong as often as they're right. But analysts have never been more valuable to the individual investor. You just have to know how to use them.

Sometimes data are useful for more than just their intended purpose. For example, I have a theory about picking wines from a restaurant menu when you're undecided between two types and the brands are unfamiliar. Suppose your choice is between a Chianti and a Sangiovese. They're priced the same and you feel both would go well with your meal. (In fact, they're made from the same grape.) The menu contains plenty of data, including names, years, and descriptions: hints of this, notes of that, something woody, and so on. I'd pick the Sangiovese. Everyone knows how to pronounce Chianti. That means everyone feels comfortable ordering it. All that demand for easy-to-pronounce wines suggests their prices are higher for a given level of quality. Since these wines are the same price, the quality of the Sangiovese is probably higher than that of the Chianti. I should mention that I had already downed several glasses of difficult-to-pronounce wine the night I developed this theory, but the point here is that sometimes you can find uses for data that the providers didn't intend.

The analyst research reported on financial Web sites contains lots of nifty features. There are forecasts for how much companies will earn this year and next, and for the compounded rate at which their earnings will grow over the next several years. There are one-year price targets and recommendations as to whether one should buy, hold, or, in rare cases, sell shares. The best use for this data isn't always the intended one. For example, decades of research on buy, hold, and sell recommendations provide little evidence that they consistently predict the right share price movements. I use them anyway—not to decide whether to buy a stock, but to gauge a stock's popularity. If I run a search for deep value stocks, I like to avoid those with excess popularity left to lose. So I build into my screen a demand that all stocks with average recommendations of buy or strong buy be eliminated from the results. In the Surprise, Surprise screen discussed in Chapter 14, we made use of earnings and sales estimates, but not because we felt they were reliable. Rather, we looked for companies that had recently beaten them.

I call the screen we'll look at in a moment Bold Is Beautiful. It, too, makes use of analysts' earnings estimates, but not so much for what the numbers actually are as for how they're scattered.

When a financial reporter says that a particular company is expected to earn $1.50 a share this year, he or she is usually citing a consensus of all analyst estimates for which data are available. The estimates are collected by companies like Thomson First Call and Reuters Research, who then report the average estimate (the consensus), high and low estimates, any recent changes in the consensus, and more.

Scores of studies from the likes of Anna Scherbina, a Harvard professor, suggest that companies with tightly clustered earnings estimates tend to produce better stock returns than those with disperse estimates. In a paper titled "Difference of Opinion and the Cross Section of Stock Returns" published in 2002 in the *Journal of Finance,* Scherbina and two colleagues reported a whopping 9 percent a year difference in the returns generated by stocks with low estimate dispersion and high estimate dispersion. The effect was most pronounced in shares of small companies.

There are a couple of theories as to why that happens. One has to do with short selling restrictions. *Short selling* involves selling borrowed shares of a stock in hopes it will go lower. If it does, you can buy the shares at the lower price and pocket the difference. Investors are free to buy stock at any time, but before they can sell stock short, a broker must be able to locate shares for them to borrow. Also, up until a July 2007 change rule change, short sales could only be executed after what's called an *up tick*—a transaction that occurs at a higher price than the preceding one. Both rules were meant to prevent short sellers from manipulating stock prices or making panic selling worse. The latter restriction was eventually deemed unfair, since no similar rule applies to stock buyers.

Consider how short-selling restrictions might affect a stock whose earnings estimates are scattered far from the consensus. The disperse estimates suggest wide disagreement on how much the company will earn. Some investors are far more bullish than average. They're free to buy shares, thereby pushing them higher. Some investors are much more bearish. They can't always sell shares short. So the stock moves higher. Stocks with disperse earnings estimates, then, might already be overpriced and due for lackluster performance in coming years.

There's also a simpler explanation for why scattered estimates predict poor stock performance and tightly clustered estimates predict big gains. Companies that are proud of their performance are more likely to volunteer heaps of information to Wall Street analysts. More information makes for more accurate earnings forecasts. Companies with something to hide offer fewer details to analysts, leaving them guessing as to future earnings. Thus, a tighter consensus is a more confident consensus, and might signal a better company.

The aforementioned study results already have the makings of a good stock screen. Simply search among small and mid-sized companies (the estimate dispersion effect is stronger for them, recall) for tightly clustered consensuses. In stock screening parlance, that's called a *low standard deviation of estimates*. So if you want to run a search for tightly clustered estimates, you might look for standard deviations lower than, say, the S&P 500 index's median standard deviation of estimates, while focusing on companies with market values of between $500 million and $5 billion.

Before you do, though, let me share another finding on estimate dispersion that I think is even more interesting. It has to do with cases where estimates are tightly clustered, but a single analyst moves away from the herd.

An analyst who issues an earnings estimate that stands far apart from the consensus makes a daring move. They risk criticism from peers, clients, and the company whose earnings are being forecast. If they're wrong a couple of times on such lone-wolf estimates, they might even lose their jobs.

This is by no means a representative case, but Rick Whittington, a longtime semiconductor analyst who is now the head of research at Caris & Co. in New York, shared with me what must be the mother of all risk-to-issuing-a-bold-estimate stories. Whittington recommended semiconductor stocks for much of the early 1990s, and to a profitable end for his firm's clients. In the fall of 1995, he saw some worrisome signs in the industry and cautioned investors to start selling shares. Some stocks tumbled. (Whittington was right. Those stocks would move much lower over the next year.) Around Thanksgiving, the U.S. Secret Service showed up at Whittington's home. Agents had been monitoring threats made online against the president. They found plenty made against Whittington. No harm came to Whittington, but his firm hired security guards to watch his house.

Fortunately, analyst death threats are uncommon. But analysts issuing bold estimate revisions had better be sure they're right if they want to keep their jobs. New research suggests they usually are. In a 2003 paper titled "Analyst Forecast Revisions and Market Price Discovery" published in *The Accounting Review*, Cristi Gleason, now at the University of Arizona, and Charles Lee at Cornell looked at hundreds of cases of bold estimate revisions between 1993 and 1998. Keep in mind that the size of an estimate revision isn't what makes it bold. Rather, what matters is whether it moves away from the herd. If the earnings consensus for a stock stands at $1.50 a share and an analyst raises his estimate by a dime to $1.45, that's a *herding revision* because it moves closer to the consensus. If an analyst on the same stock raises the estimate by a dime to $1.65 a share, that's a *bold revision* because it moves away from the consensus.

Previous studies have established that stocks tend to slightly outperform the market over the months following a raised earnings estimate—in much the same way they tend to drift higher after upside earnings surprises, as discussed during our look at the Surprise, Surprise strategy. Gleason and Lee set out to see how stocks react following bold estimate revisions. They simulated buying stocks immediately following bold estimate increases and selling them short immediately following bold estimate reductions. Their strategy beat the market by a stunning 15 percentage points a year.

A follow-up to that study, published in 2005 in the *Journal of Finance*, offered evidence as to why the strategy works so well. Bold estimate increases predict bigger stock gains than herding ones because the bold ones tend to be more accurate about future earnings. Analysts, it seems, tend to step away from the herd only when they have good reason to do so.

Time to screen. You'll need a powerful stock screener, and you'll have to do a bit of manual sorting with the results. There's no way I know of to specify that you want to search only for estimate revisions that step away from the consensus, but you can come close. Focus on companies worth between $500 million and $5 billion. Look for stocks that have been the subject of exactly one estimate increase in the past week and none during the few weeks before that. That shows that one analyst has turned more bullish without any influence from peers or widely reported company news. When you have your list of companies, cross check them on a financial Web site that details not just consensus changes but changes in each individual estimate that makes up the consensus. Look up the details on each changed estimate. Note the price it started at and the price it moved to. Check this information against the consensus estimate for the company, and you should be able to tell whether it was a bold or a herding revision. It might take a half hour or so of grunt work, but think of it as a half hour of effort that keeps lazy investors from capturing your stock profits.

The Bold Is Beautiful Screen Recipe

- Market value between $500 million and $5 billion
- Exactly one current-year earnings estimate increase within past week
- Exactly one current-year earnings estimate increase within past four weeks
- Past-week increase in current-year earnings estimate in top 25 percent for industry

Remember, these clues won't tell you whether the estimate increase was bold or herding. You'll have to look into that yourself.

Chapter 18

The Rising Expectations Screen

Never get on an empty New York City subway car when all the other cars are full. The empty car isn't a sign of your good fortune. It's a sign that either the air conditioning is broken or that someone has done something unpleasant enough to make everyone leave.

That's an example of advice that doesn't expire. You can use it today or a year from now. Not so, analyst recommendations. Those are best used fresh, or not at all.

I've noted throughout the book that analyst buy recommendations generally aren't worth following. Yet some studies suggest otherwise. One found that during the 10 years ended 1996, stocks with strong buy ratings outperformed those with strong sell ratings by 13 percentage points a year.

Look through the stack of contradictory findings on the subject, and two common points emerge. First, sell recommendations are better predictors of poor stock performance than buy recommendations are of good performance. That makes sense. Analysts are loath to advise investors to sell stocks. Most firms issue anywhere from 3 to 15 times as many buy recommendations as sell recommendations. A cynical investor would blame that on conflict of interest. Recall that investment firms try to sell services to the same companies their analysts rate. There's a benign explanation, though. Analysts look for stocks worth buying because that's what account holders at their firms are interested in.

So there's probably money to be made in following sell recommendations if you're into short selling or buying put options. This book is about finding your next great stock, though, not your next lousy one.

The second common point that turns up in the research on analyst recommendations is that buys outperform when the market is strong and underperform when it's weak. Buy-rated stocks underperformed sell-rated ones in 2000 and 2001, for example. That's because analysts show a strong preference for popular stocks, or what Wall Street calls *growth stocks*. Recall from Chapter 11 that growth stocks tend to outperform during strong markets, underperform during weak ones, and perform in line with the market over long time periods.

Whether following buy ratings will pay off, then, depends on what kind of market you're in. But there are a couple of things you can do to swing the odds sharply in your favor.

First, search for ratings improvements, rather than for ratings that are flattering but stagnant. Stocks tend to outperform the broad market after analysts turn sweeter on them, whether those analysts are raising their ratings to hold from sell or to buy from hold.

You've probably seen a stock jump on the day an analyst gives it a buy rating. That's not the kind of outperformance I'm talking about. Such reactions happen too quickly for most investors to take advantage of them. (Take advantage of them legally, that is. In March 2007, a ring of 13 managers, traders, and compliance officers working for several renowned investment firms had been charged in connection with trading illegally on foreknowledge of recommendation changes. It started with an investment bank executive working off a $25,000 debt to a money manager friend by tipping him the day before recommendation changes.

Brokers and compliance officials caught on to the abnormal trading patterns. Rather than report them, they allegedly duplicated the trades in their own accounts or demanded bribes to stay quiet. Prosecutors said the ring made more than $15 million in illegal profits.)

There are longer-term returns to favoring stocks with recent ratings upgrades, according to a paper titled "Analysts, Industries and Price Momentum," published in 2006 in the *Journal of Financial and Quantitative Analysis*. (I only read it for the sexy photos.) Kent Womack, an investment banker turned Dartmouth professor, and Leslie Boni, who teaches at the University of New Mexico, looked at 100,000 changes in analyst recommendations between 1996 and 2002, a period that included great and awful years for the stock market. Changes, they found, were far more useful for stock-picking purposes than whether the average recommendation was positive. The two simulated purchasing buy-rated stocks while selling sell-rated ones. Returns over the next month were unimpressive. Then the two simulated buying stocks that had been upgraded in the previous month while selling ones that had been downgraded. Returns averaged 1.23 percent over the following month. Annualized, that works out to nearly 15 percent a year, six percentage points more than the broad market's return during the study period. (The data set excluded stocks priced under $5 a share. Returns to a different data set that included such stocks were even better.)

The strong performance is likely related to the freshness of the recommendations. At any given time, the opinions that make up a consensus recommendation may be six months old or older. By looking for recommendation changes, you're looking for fresh advice.

Putting the aforementioned strategy into practice would be difficult. An investor would have to make heaps of trades each month, and the study returns didn't take out for trading fees or taxes. Still, the research suggests that if you're looking for great stocks, analyst upgrades can give you an edge. Womack and Boni, keep in mind, looked for revisions over the past month. You can look for them over the past week, which should make the advice even fresher and thereby improve its predictive power.

There's a second thing you can do to boost your returns even further. Look for the most-upgraded stocks in the most-upgraded industries. In the same study, Womack and Boni changed their approach in order to study industry momentum. They divided the companies into 59 different industry portfolios. Then they simulated buying only upgraded stocks in industries that had received more upgrades than downgrades, while selling only downgraded stocks in industries that had received more downgrades than upgrades. Returns swelled to 1.41 percent the following month, or 17 percent a year.

Again, you'll want to hold your stocks for longer than the one-month period used in the Womack and Boni study. But the broad point still applies. By searching for stock bargains among recently upgraded companies in recently upgraded industries, you'll significantly improve your chances of finding winners.

You'll need a capable stock screener like the Zacks Research Wizard for this screen, and you'll have to do a little manual sorting of the screen results, but that part is easy. I'd exclude giant companies from your search universe, since smaller ones tend to react more to analyst upgrades. Screen for stocks with more upgrades than downgrades over the past week. Then export the results to Excel. With the Zacks screener the stocks will already be grouped by industry, which makes the next part easier. If you're using a different screener, be sure to display each company's industry in your report, and then sort the stocks by industry from within Excel.

Next, determine which industries had the most net upgrades (upgrades minus downgrades). You can go through and calculate the average number of net upgrades for each industry, but you might not have to bother. The last time I ran this screen, focusing on companies with market values of $200 million to $10 billion, I got just under 100 screen survivors. That's a short enough list to allow you to glance down the table and see which industries have the most upgrades, as well as which stocks within those industries have the most upgrades.

I won't bother listing the recipe for this screen. It consists of only two clues—company size and number of net upgrades—and I don't want the reader who skips ahead to the recipes to think that's all there is to the screen. The most important part is the quick sorting by industry you do after you get the results.

Chapter 19

The Follow the Leaders Screen

Imagine you had a giant Rolodex with the names and phone numbers of all of America's top bosses. Imagine, too, that all of them were willing to take your calls. Instead of relying on the opinions of outsiders when deciding whether to buy a company's shares, you could dial up the person who knows the company best. "Shoot me straight," you could say. "Are your shares a bargain at this price?"

Having chatted with a number of chief executives in the course of writing about their stocks, I'm convinced your giant Rolodex wouldn't do much for your investment results. The above question, for one thing, is always going to elicit one of two responses. The first one is "yes." The second is "I don't comment on the stock price, but. . ." followed by a long list of positives that amount to a "yes." The other problem with top bosses is that almost all of them in one of their former jobs sold something, and sold it well. They're too convincing. You don't want to take stock advice from someone who always says "buy" and has a knack for talking you into it.

That's what I like about stock screening. Screening software doesn't care whether a company's boss is a real go-getter. It only cares about what he or she has gone and gotten. You already have access to two things that are far more important to your stock returns than an in-person pitch from the chief executive. The first is the company's financial reports, which lay out the case without the fluff. The second is the most reliable indicator I've found of whether a boss truly thinks their stock is a good buy: the number of shares they've bought for themselves in recent months.

That information isn't difficult to find. Top executives are part of a class of investors called *insiders*. Other insiders include a company's board members and its so-called *beneficial owners*—those with more than a 10 percent stake in the stock. Financial reporters generally use the term *insider trading* only when referring to nefarious activity, but the overwhelming majority of insider trades are perfectly legal. Insiders may buy and sell their company shares as they like, so long as they follow a few rules.

One of the rules requires that insiders report their trades to the public almost immediately after making them. They must fill out a Form 4 within two business days of executing the trade. The form doesn't tell the public why an insider bought or sold shares, but it contains plenty of other useful information. It lists the name of the insider and his or her relationship to the company, the trade date, the number of shares involved, the price at which the trade was executed, and the number of shares the insider owns following the trade. It also includes a letter that indicates the type of trade. "P" is a regular purchase and "S" is a regular sale. (The SEC calls it an "open market or private purchase/sale of [a] non-derivative or derivative security.") There are 18 other codes for everything from gifts to option exercises.

Form 4s used to be filed through the mail. Today they're filed through the Electronic Data Gathering Analysis and Retrieval System, lovingly known as *Edgar*. Anyone with an Internet connection has access to Edgar. You'll find links to the system on the SEC's Web site. Simply type in a stock symbol and you can view all documents the company has filed in recent years, including Form 4s.

You can also run a general search for companies whose insiders are buying by using a stock screener. Data collectors like Hemscott and Thomson Financial strip the information off Form 4s and other filings as soon as they hit the Edgar database and distribute it to financial Web sites and other customers. It used to take weeks to learn that an insider had bought shares. Today, if a company's boss buys shares on Tuesday, there's a good chance the trade will turn up on a screen you run on Thursday.

You'd be wise to run such a screen now and again. Top executives have a knack for buying their company's shares at the right moment. One long-term study published a few years ago concluded that, on average, they beat the broad stock market by six percentage points a year.

There's a tidy explanation for the investment performance of insiders and a not-so-tidy one. The tidy one is that they simply have a better understanding than the rest of us of the long-term growth prospects for their industries and their companies. The not-so-tidy one is that they see things we don't.

That's a tricky subject. One of the most important rules insiders must adhere to requires that they abstain from trading based on information that is both material and nonpublic. *Material* means the information is the sort of thing that would affect a stock's price, like the test results for an experimental drug. *Nonpublic,* of course, means only those closest to the company are privy to the information. It's perfectly acceptable for a boss to buy his company shares based on drug trial results reported yesterday. It's a crime, though, to buy them based on results that will be reported tomorrow.

There are plenty of gray areas. For example, if an executive notices that phones in the sales department suddenly started ringing incessantly last week, is that *material* information? If the boss knows his marketing director is going through an ugly divorce that's affecting his job performance, is that *nonpublic?* I'd love to believe that insiders never place trades on information the rest of us don't have access to. But that's unrealistic.

Fortunately for those of us trying to profit from insider trades, following the rules is their concern, not ours. Even in the case of an insider buy that's based on nonpublic information, the transaction itself is public information once it hits the Edgar database. So feel free to follow-up insider buys with your own purchases anytime you like.

A few words of advice before you do: The aforementioned stock returns of insiders are high because a relatively few of them achieve stellar results. But you're not going to buy every stock that has been the subject of insider buying. More likely, you'll choose one or two of them. That makes things tricky. If you randomly select a single boss's purchase to mimic, a recent Morgan Stanley study suggests your chance of beating the broad market is only a little better than even odds.

You can improve your results dramatically by looking for the right kind of insider buying. Citibank's quantitative strategies department in London (people who look for ways to beat the market using stock screens, essentially) recently developed some ideas on how to do that. In 2006 the group studied 9,000 insider transactions made in the United Kingdom since 1994. They looked for common traits among purchases that went on to produce the highest returns. They found plenty.

Bigger purchases tended to predict better stock returns. That makes sense. The more money insiders spend on shares, the more confident they presumably are. But the group also found that the relationship between purchase size and returns reverses once purchases become too large as a percentage of outstanding shares. One possible explanation: Investors get worried when they see a boss trying to buy his or her way into long-term entrenchment.

Executive purchases did better than those made by board members or major shareholders. (All count as insiders for reporting purposes, recall.) Prior studies have shown the same thing. This, too, makes sense. Board members and big shareholders (often investment funds) share an obvious interest in the company's operations, but executives are the ones who actually run companies from day to day. Also, investment funds spend other people's money, and board members are sometimes required to buy shares as part of their contracts. Executives buy shares voluntarily, and always reach into their own pockets to do so. (The Sarbanes–Oxley act of 2002 put an end to the shady practice of executives borrowing company money to buy its shares.)

Purchases by several executives within the past three months tended to produce better performance in the Citibank study than purchases by one. Insider purchases at small companies with limited analyst coverage fared particularly well. The right mix of stock attributes also gave a big boost to results. Buys that followed upside earnings surprises did well. So did purchases of stocks with modest valuations, judging by metrics like the price/earnings ratio. Finally, stocks with strong price performance over the 260 days leading up to an insider purchase paid off particularly well.

Most of these findings are easy to build into a stock screen, but you'll have to do a little bit of manual sorting after you produce your results. SmartMoney.com's stock quote pages offer an insider buying chart you may find useful for your research. It plots transactions using green for purchases, red for sales, and different sizes depending on the dollar amounts involved. It shows at a glance the stock's recent trading and the buy and sell points, which allows you to make sure the insider purchases were made at the same prices available to the rest of us.

Insiders sell shares more often than they buy them. Some investors like to look for companies with net insider buying—more buying than selling. I don't. Studies show that selling is far less predictive of stock performance than buying. Most executives, after all, receive stock as part of their compensation. They have to sell shares from time to time to pay for, say, a new gold liner for their dollar-sign-shaped swimming pool filled with tears of the working class (according to my union manual). So run screens based on buying alone, and pay attention to sales afterward only in cases where you see rampant selling by more than one executive.

Keep in mind that many executives, seeking to protect themselves from charges of timing the market based on inside information, set up automatic selling programs. If you see sales at regular intervals and dollar amounts by the same executive, they're probably happening automatically. Also, look out for cases where an executive buys and sells equal-size blocks of shares on the same day. That's someone moving stock from one account to another, and it's hardly reason to get excited about a company's investment prospects.

Follow the Leaders Screen Recipe

- Dollars spent on insider purchases greater than $100,000
- Shares purchased by insiders less than 5 percent of outstanding shares
- Number of insider buys greater than or equal to 2

- Market value less than $10 billion
- Number of analysts in current-year earnings consensus less than or equal to six

Remember to check to see which insiders are buying. Executive purchases are the most promising. Further reduce your list by adding other promising signs that turned up in the Citibank study.

- Price/earnings ratio below industry average
- Six-month share price gain greater than S&P 500 gain

Chapter 20

The Accrual to Be Kind Screen

My barber doesn't need an accountant to figure out how much money he makes. He uses something called *cigar box accounting*. It requires nothing more than an empty cigar box and the ability to count. The cigar box is optional.

The money he collects for each haircut ($10 plus tip) goes into the box. Once in a while money for supplies—cans of talcum powder that look like they sold well in Hoover's day or the mysterious blue liquid the combs swim in—comes out of the box. At the end of each day, the money he has in the box, minus the few dollars he started with, is profit. Ask my barber how much he earned in a given day and he'll point to the box. Ask him how much free cash he generated, and he'll keep pointing.

Ask a publicly traded company how much it earned last quarter and how much free cash it generated, and you'll likely get two different answers. In what follows, I'll explain where the difference between those answers comes from, and how you can use it to do two important things. You can look through stocks you already own for signs of trouble. You can also search the entire market for stocks that look likely to produce plentiful returns.

Earnings aren't real. When a company says it earned $1 per share last quarter, it doesn't mean that it added that much to the cigar box. It might have added more or less. It might have added nothing. Suppose it added 70 cents. The difference between the $1 it earned and the 70 cents it has to show for those earnings comes from what accountants call *accruals*. You can think of them as "yeahbuts." They represent a company saying things like, "Yeah, but we would have made more if our customers didn't take so long to pay." Or, "Yeah, but if you don't count the money we spent on that new factory, our profits were great."

Accruals aren't necessarily bad. In fact, companies are required to use them when reporting their earnings. That's because tallying profits is just one of the goals of corporate accounting. The other is to tell a good story.

Suppose my barber decides to start accepting credit cards, and half his customers start using them. He usually adds $2,000 a week to his cigar box, but now he only adds $1,000 in cash, and receives the rest from the credit card companies a month or so after each sale. I stop in and ask how business is going. He could say he only added $1,000 to the box last week instead of his usual $2,000. That's accurate, but it doesn't really reflect the pace of his business. So long as he's confident the other $1,000 is coming soon from the credit card companies, better to say he earned $2,000 than focus on how much he actually collected.

Stock investors tend to focus largely on the pace of a company's business. They want to know if it's bringing in more customers and writing up more sales, and if it's clearing healthy profits as a result of those sales. For that reason, they usually look first at the quarterly income statement. It's tallied using what's called *accrual accounting*. Income is counted as it's accrued (but not necessarily collected) and expenses are subtracted as they're incurred (but not necessarily paid).

Lenders tend to focus on how much cash is coming in. They want to know whether a company will be able to make its loan payments after paying all its other expenses. So they go straight for the quarterly cash flow statement. It tracks cash coming in and going out, without regard to when sales were agreed on.

The *matching principle* plays a large part in creating accruals, or the difference between a company's income statement and its cash flow statement. Recall from Chapter 15 that the matching principle states that, when possible, companies should pair expenses with sales that it makes as a result of those expenses. The cost of manufacturing a shovel, for example, should be subtracted on the income statement in the same quarter that shovel is sold. By doing that, companies give investors a clear picture of the returns they achieve on the money they spend. The income statement makes it look like the expenses were paid in the same quarter the returns were received. Of course, that's not necessarily the case. The cash flow statement shows how much money actually changed hands that quarter.

The aforementioned examples show current accruals, which result largely from a company's timing of payments in its day-to-day business. Sometimes companies create long-term accruals. Suppose my barber buys a new chair for $5,000. Once again, I stop in and ask how business is going. He made $2,000 this week, but he also bought the chair. He could tell me he lost $3,000, but that wouldn't accurately reflect how things are going. He could ignore the chair purchase, but that wouldn't be right, either. It was, after all, money he paid to grow his business. So he decides to pretend he's paying for the chair little by little, even thought he already bought it. He figures the chair should be good for at least five years of haircuts. Its $5,000 cost paid weekly over five years works out to about $19 a week. So he tells me he made $1,981 that week, or his $2,000 minus one week's worth of cost for the chair.

Companies do something similar on their income statements. They use processes called *depreciation* and *amortization* to pretend that big-ticket purchases they paid for in the past are being made little by little each quarter. Depreciation gradually charges off the cost of tangible items like plants and equipment, while amortization does the same for intangible items like brands and patents. Accounting laws dictate the time period companies should use for each good, depending on the projected useful life of that good—five years for cars, for example.

Depreciation and amortization allow companies to spend large sums to expand their businesses—often more than they make in a quarter—without worrying that investors will view them as suddenly losing money. When we say a manufacturer grew profits by 15 percent last year, we might mean that it did so while pretending it didn't shell out all that money at once for the new plant it bought.

These examples of accruals are perfectly legitimate ones. They make things clearer for stock investors, and for that reason companies are required to use accrual accounting on their income statements. Sometimes accruals can cover up shady dealings, though.

Managers of publicly traded companies face enormous pressure to *hit their numbers*—to report profits each quarter that are at least as good as those Wall Street is forecasting. They face several types of punishment if they fail to do so. First, their share prices might fall. That makes shareholders angry and reduces the value of stock positions that managers hold for themselves. Second, managers' bonuses are sometimes paid according to the profits they produce.

Good managers use all that incentive to run their companies well. Bad ones fail to do so and are hopefully paid accordingly or even dismissed. Dishonest managers, though, can use accruals to make things look great for a few quarters, cash in on their bonuses and stock gains, and leave before anyone realizes the damage they've done. Such managers are few. Their tactics have largely been made illegal. And high-profile accounting scandals like those at Enron and WorldCom have resulted in increased scrutiny of corporate accounting practices. So hopefully these activities are becoming less common. But let's look at a couple of examples anyway.

Suppose a maker of toy fire trucks is suffering from slow sales during what should be its peak selling season—the run-up to Christmas. Desperate to move more merchandise, the boss instructs the sales team to call the big retail toy chains and offer cut-rate financing for those that place huge orders. The stores don't really need that many trucks, but the terms of the offer are too tempting to pass up. So they buy all the trucks they are likely to sell that year rather than just that quarter. The manufacturer books all of those orders as sales and reports a great Christmas season. Investors are pleased. The boss gets a big bonus. All is well until the following quarter, when the manufacturer is unable to sell any trucks because stores already have more than they can use.

That practice is called *channel stuffing*. In effect, it steals sales from future quarters to make the current quarter look better. It's particularly dangerous for investors. Since channel stuffing flatters current results, it tends to attract a rush of stock buyers just before things turn sour.

Financing terms aren't the only tools companies can use to artificially inflate their sales. They can also offer generous return privileges. That same toymaker might tell stores that if they placed big orders and some of the trucks don't sell, they can simply return them for a refund. That's a great deal for the stores, who usually run the risk of being stuck with too much inventory if a product flops. Again, they buy big and the Christmas season looks like a huge success. But in future quarters the trucks start coming back and sales suffer.

Some businesses depend on generous return privileges. Bookstores, for example, can stock a vast number of books only because publishers agree to take back the ones that don't sell. But such businesses use special accounting measures to compensate. Publishers don't count all the books they ship to stores as sales right away. They make adjustments for the number of books that are likely to be returned. When a company offers exaggerated return privileges without adjusting for them in recording its sales, it does so to inflate its returns and deceive its shareholders.

Those tactics affect sales. There are plenty of underhanded ways to boost earnings, too. One illegal way is to mislabel an expense as a capital investment. Expenses are things like advertising spending, salaries, and the electricity bill at a company's headquarters. They're day-to-day costs, and so are subtracted from sales right away on a company's income statements. Capital investments are big-ticket purchases like plants and equipment. They qualify for depreciation. Expenses reduce profits right away, but capital investments do so little by little over a long time periods. Accounting rules are pretty clear about what qualifies as a capital investment and what doesn't. Unscrupulous managers who break the rules reduce current expenses, thereby inflating profits.

Don't panic. Such tactics are rarely used. Most accruals occur for perfectly legitimate reasons. Still, think about treating all companies with accruals as guilty, even though they're not. By separating companies with mostly paper profits from those that bring in plenty of cash, you can find great stocks.

A decade ago Richard Sloan, an accounting professor at the University of Michigan, discovered something important about accruals and published the details in *The Accounting Review,* an academic journal. The paper is titled "Do Stock Prices Fully Reflect Information in Accruals and Cash Flows About Future Earnings?" Companies with small or negative accruals, Sloan found, tend to produce far better stock returns than those with large ones. He created a portfolio simulation that bought shares of companies with negative accruals while selling short shares of companies with positive ones. Between 1962 and 1991 it outperformed the broad market by 10 percentage points a year.

Sloan's study considered only current accruals—those that arise mostly due to the timing of payments and expenses. His results make sense intuitively. Positive accruals flatter earnings. They make a company look suddenly more profitable, even though it's not necessarily growing its business. Since investors often focus on earnings at the expense of cash flows, companies whose earnings are inflated by accruals might have inflated share prices to match. Companies with negative accruals, meanwhile, might be underappreciated. Their earnings have been temporarily obscured. By purchasing shares of companies with hidden earnings rather than those of companies with inflated ones, investors ought to be able to outperform the market.

A few years ago, Sloan and two colleagues published a follow-up study in the *Journal of Accounting and Economics* titled "Accrual Reliability, Earnings Persistence and Stock Prices." It looked at all accruals, not just current ones. That is, it looked at companies whose earnings were altered by timing-of-payment issues and by whether large purchases were classified as expenses or capital investments, among other things. It set up a similar portfolio simulation and generated equally impressive results. It also found that companies with high accruals tend to produce poor earnings going forward—likely the reason for their poor stock performance.

The math that study used to calculate accruals was easy. It simply subtracted free cash flow from earnings and called the difference *total net operating accruals*. A negative number meant the stock should be bought because part of its earnings were hidden. A positive number meant the stock should be sold because its earnings were inflated.

Since Sloan's original study, institutional investors have put his findings—now called the *accrual anomaly*—to profitable use. Hedge funds now look closely at accruals, both to find bargain stocks to buy and to avoid or sell short the next WorldCom. (That company's accrual abuse of choice was misclassifying expenses as capital investments, although management dabbled in just making up sales, too.) Of course, when too many investors know about a strategy and exploit it, the strategy tends to disappear. That is, if everyone knows stocks with hidden earnings might be bargains, they'll buy them and run the share prices up, leaving no more bargains. But as recently as 2006 a study published in the *Financial Analysts Journal* titled "Cash Flows, Accruals and Future Returns" and written by Joshua Livnat, an NYU accounting professor, and Massimo Santicchia, a director at Standard and Poor's Investment Services, documented that the accrual anomaly is still going strong. The study sought merely to see if companies' most recent quarterly results were as useful as their most recent annual ones (which Sloan had used) for finding bargains based on accruals. Its accrual-based strategy beat the market by more than nine percentage points a year.

The accrual anomaly tends to be far stronger for small and medium-sized companies. That's a clue as to why institutional investors have failed to trade the strategy away. They focus mainly on large companies with a high volume of shares traded each day. Your best chance of finding bargains, then, might be to look for negative accruals among smaller companies that don't attract as many professional investors.

To calculate a company's accruals you'll need to know its earnings and free cash flow. Earnings, of course, are listed at the end of a company's income statement. *Free cash flow* isn't listed on financial statements, but it's not difficult to calculate. Start with earnings, add back in any deductions that were made for depreciation and amortization, and subtract any capital investments. That reverses the effect of a company breaking down its big-ticket purchases into smaller quarterly amounts. Next, adjust for any changes in working capital, or current assets minus current liabilities, during the period for which you're calculating free cash flow. That erases the effects of the timing-of-payment issues. The resulting figure is free cash flow.

Of course, you don't have to do the math to run the screen. Simply use a stock screener that allows you to search for both earnings and free cash flow and allows you to build your own formulas. Look for smaller companies with plenty of earnings and negative accruals. Further reduce your list of screen survivors by making demands on stock valuations and earnings growth potential.

The Accrual to Be Kind Screen Recipe

- Trailing 12-month free cash flow minus trailing 12-month net income greater than zero
- Market value between $200 million and $10 billion
- Three-year annualized earnings growth greater than 15 percent
- One-year earnings growth greater than three-year annualized earnings growth
- Price/earnings ratio below industry median

Chapter 21

The Sales on Sale Screen

Sometimes two or more measures of a stock's value disagree on whether it's cheap. A stock's price/earnings ratio might say it is a bargain, while its price/cash flow ratio says the opposite. The same goes for measures like price/free-cash-flow, price/book value, price/sales, EV/EBITDA, and others we looked at in Chapter 10.

That raises the question of which one is right most often. If the measures sometimes disagree, after all, some must be better than others at predicting stock gains.

Two of the measures, in fact, stand out as having an astounding record of beating the market when mixed in with the right supporting clues. Neither gets nearly as much attention as the P/E ratio, despite ample evidence that shows they produce better results. They're the price/sales ratio and the price/book-value ratio. We'll look at a strategy based on the first one in this chapter and one based on the second one in Chapter 22.

Sales might seem like an unlikely candidate for a powerful predictor of stock gains. They appear at the top of a company's income statement. That means they say nothing about whether the company is profitable. A company might be selling plenty of goods and services but at prices that don't exceed its costs. And because sales are on the income statement, they don't tell you whether a company is producing cash, either. A company might be writing up plenty of product orders but not collecting the payments.

Yet sales have a few advantages over more comprehensive measures like earnings and free cash flow. Free cash flow can spike or plummet, based on whether a company invests in big, income-producing assets such as plants and equipment in a given quarter. Not so, sales. Earnings are subject to a large amount of accounting subjectivity, which means they can sometimes be made to look more flattering than they should. Sales are far more difficult to manipulate.

Fast-growing companies often post rapid sales increases long before they perfect their margins. So sales might give earlier notice than earnings that things are going well for a young company. Also, the P/S ratio may benefit from its lack of popularity relative to the P/E ratio. Since most investors hunt for low-P/E stocks, those who search for low-P/S bargains have less competition.

The price/sales ratio is calculated by dividing a company's current stock price by a year's worth of its sales. Generally those sales come from the trailing 12-month period, although I suppose you could use the current fiscal year forecast if you wanted to create a forward P/S ratio.

Two people helped bring the P/S ratio to the attention of ordinary investors. Kenneth Fisher, a long-time *Forbes* columnist and the head of Fisher Investments, a California money management firm, made a case for the usefulness of the measure in his 1984 book *Super Stocks*. Also, James O'Shaughnessy, now a strategist for Bear Stearns, called price/sales "the king of the value factors" in his 1996 book detailing his search for the best stock performance predictors, called *What Works on Wall Street*.

O'Shaughnessy found that $10,000 invested in high-P/S (expensive) stocks in 1951 turned into just over $19,000 by 2003, while the same amount invested in low-P/S (cheap) stocks turned into more than $22 million over the same period. Low-P/S stocks produced annual returns of about 16 percent a year, about three percentage points a year better than all stocks and more than two percentage points better than low-P/E stocks. Further tweaking the strategy, O'Shaughnessy found that by combining low P/S ratios with demands for earnings growth and share price momentum, investors during his study period would have earned returns of more than 18 percent a year, enough to turn that $10,000 into $53 million.

You can find great stocks by running periodic searches for low P/S ratios and other promising signs. One thing that gives this screen an advantage over earnings-based ones is that it isn't dependent on analyst coverage. If you run a screen for companies with low forward P/Es, you'll restrict your search to companies for which analysts have issued earnings estimates. Since the P/S ratio usually looks at trailing sales, which all companies have, you might turn up some stocks that Wall Street hasn't yet caught on to.

The Sales on Sale Screen Recipe

- Trailing 12-month sales greater than $200 million
- Average daily trading volume greater than 100,000 shares
- Price/sales ratio below 1.5
- Past-year earnings growth positive
- Three-month share price appreciation greater than database average
- Six-month share price appreciation greater than database average

O'Shaughnessy calls this recipe his *Cornerstone Growth* strategy, and recommends buying the 50 screen survivors with highest one-year price appreciation. If you're looking for one or two great stocks rather than following the 50-stock strategy, you might reduce the number of screen survivors by increasing the earnings-growth demand and adding a demand for sales growth, too.

Chapter 22

The Combination Platter Screen

People I work with sometimes marvel that my desk looks completely empty every day. It's not, of course. On top are a computer and a telephone. Inside is a big-button calculator. Next to it, for emergencies, are one pen and a pad of paper. But that's it.

There's no inspirational calendar. There's no calendar that satirizes inspirational calendars. There's no baseball or bobble-head doll. I keep only what I need, which, since I make words for a living, is just about nothing.

Corporate America is, in a way, becoming more like me. It's not that workers are adopting my Spartan approach at their desks. It's that fewer of us are welding axles and sewing shoe leather for a living, and more of us are just sitting around thinking stuff up. That's called *an information economy,* and it has made things trickier for stock pickers.

Thirty years ago the average company's book value, or what accountants say it would fetch by selling off its assets, was just 5 percent shy of its market value, or what the stock market said the whole company was worth. In other words, investors expected companies to have plants and hard assets, and were willing to pay only a smidgen more than the net value of those assets when buying shares. Today the average company's book value is well less than half its market value.

What are investors paying for? They're buying intellectual property such as copyrights and patents. They're buying brands, which allow companies to charge higher prices for their products. They're buying things like good customer relations, which presumably bode well for future sales. All of these things are called *intangible assets*. If you buy shares of Coca-Cola, you're not buying them because the company has somehow proved more effective than any other in the world at mixing water, gas, corn sugar, and flavoring. It's not the manufacturing that makes the money. It's the way the company convinces people to prefer Coke over other brands. Coke is in the image business.

Thirty years ago, finding cheap stocks was as easy as looking for companies that were trading for substantially less than their asset values. Today, investors prefer to look for companies that are cheap relative to the streams of income that come out of those assets and all the intangible ones. They use the price/earnings, price/sales, and price/free-cash-flow ratios, among others. And they mostly ignore the price/book ratio.

That's a mistake. There's good reason to believe a screen based on the price/book ratio can help you resoundingly beat the broad market's returns. Recall that low P/B ratios were so good at predicting generous stock returns that the measure helped "break" the original stock pricing formula, the Capital Asset Pricing Model, which said returns were a function of past volatility. That led Eugene Fama and Kenneth French in 1992 to augment the formula by acknowledging that P/B ratios and company size predict returns, too.

A University of Chicago accounting professor named Joseph Piotroski studied low-P/B stocks for the 20 years ended 1996 and detailed the results in a 2000 paper published in the *Journal of Accounting Research,* titled "Value Investing: The Use of Historical Financial Statement Information to Separate Winners from Losers." Piotroski found that low-P/B stocks beat the broad stock market by six percentage points a year, an amount more or less in line with what other studies had shown. But he noticed something troubling about how the returns were distributed. Fewer than half the stocks contributed just about all the gains. That makes things risky for ordinary investors since, unlike studies, which can track thousands of low-P/B stocks, investors would buy only a handful of them. So Piotroski set out to find ways to improve the returns.

He found plenty of indicators—nine in total, which is why I call this the Combination Platter screen. He ranked stocks on a scale from zero to nine according to how many of these attributes they displayed. Companies with the highest scores produced returns more than twice as large as the average low-P/B stocks, beating the market by 13 percentage points a year.

Four of the nine criteria call for profitability. Companies receive a point if they have positive earnings, not counting one-time charges and credits. They get another point if those earnings are growing. If operating cash flow, or the cash that companies collect as a result of their day-to-day business, is positive, they get another point. Finally, they get a point if operating cash flow is greater than earnings. Note that this last criterion is essentially the same one we looked for in Chapter 20 on the Accrual to Be Kind screen—more cash profits than paper profits.

Next are three financial strength demands. If long-term debt is falling relative to assets, companies get a point. If current assets are increasing relative to current liabilities (a sign customers are paying sooner), they get another point. They also get a point if they're not issuing stock to raise money.

The last two demands look at efficiency. Companies get a point if their gross margins are increasing and another if their asset turns—sales divided by assets—are increasing. Rising asset turns, remember, suggests management has figured out how to sell more goods or services using the resources it already has.

Stock screeners generally won't let you set up a nine-point system they way Piotroski did. And if you search for all nine items, you may find that you're left with no screen survivors. Give it a shot and monitor how small the list of survivors becomes with each new criterion you add. You may have to make a compromise or two. For example, instead of searching for debt levels that are falling relative to assets, you might try looking for those that are staying the same or falling, which would add companies with no debt to your results.

The Combination Platter Screen Recipe

- Price/book value in bottom 25 percent for database
- Trailing 12-month earnings (excluding one-time items) positive
- Trailing 12-month earnings (excluding one-time items) growing
- Trailing 12-month operating cash flow positive
- Trailing 12-month operating cash flow greater than trailing 12-month earnings
- Debt/assets ratio lower in most recent quarter than in year-ago quarter
- Current ratio (current assets/current liabilities) in most recent quarter greater than in year-ago quarter
- Net share issuance not positive
- Trailing 12-month gross margin greater than prior 12-month gross margin
- Trailing 12-month asset turns greater than prior 12-month asset turns

Chapter 23

Guru Screens

We've now looked at 11 stock screens you can run for yourself anytime. Each satisfies the five requirements of reliable stock-picking strategies set out earlier in the book. There's ample evidence that the strategies produce fat returns. There's a good explanation for why they produce those returns. The strategies have been rigorously tested for lurking variables; many of them were tested using the three-factor model to adjust their returns for the effects of volatility, value, and company size. The strategies are fairly easy to follow without sentencing yourself to sitting in front of a trading monitor all day. And finally, they fit into the language of stock screening software, albeit some more neatly than others.

You might not have recognized many of the names associated with finding these strategies. Most are applied finance types: people who alternate between developing strategies in academic settings and putting those strategies to work for investment companies. But what about the world's most renowned stock pickers, such as Warren Buffet and Peter Lynch? Where are the strategies based on their work?

There are plenty such strategies. They're called *guru screens*, and they're available on many of the financial Web sites whose stock screening tools we looked at earlier. Is running a guru screen a good idea? Perhaps, but there are some important things to keep in mind if you do.

First, there's no mystery to what makes a great stock picker. Great stock pickers review hundreds or thousands of companies looking for the right mix of clues, often using stock-screening software, or using staffs of researchers who use stock-screening software. A good guru screen, then, is a screen that's based on good clues, not one that has a popular name attached to it.

Second, a guru screen isn't really based directly on a guru's methods. It's based on someone's speculation as to what those methods are. Sometimes that's a difficult thing to guess. Some investors, for example, keep their stock-picking methods private, releasing only the occasional hint. Others write books on their approaches, but discuss methods that can't be plugged into stock-screening software because they rely more on human judgment than searchable quantities. So guru screens won't always be accurate in terms of resembling screens those investors would run for themselves. They can be inaccurate and still work, though, as long as they're based on good clues.

Third, the stock screens that great investors run are important to their results, but there are other important factors, too. Successful investors thoroughly research the companies that turn up on those screens, looking for many of the things you'll look for in the next chapter when you start your postscreen research. They also make better decisions about when to sell stocks.

Fourth, many of the investment returns you'll see attributed to guru screens on the Internet are tallied using back testing without any kind of adjustment for things like companies that went out of business or hidden variables. These screens haven't been put through the same rigorous testing as those we've looked at thus far. That doesn't mean they're not useful. As long as you're looking for some variation on the promising company attributes we looked at in Chapter 10—growing companies, well-managed companies, cheap shares, and so on—you'll likely get a better result than if you had selected stocks at random. For example, the price/sales ratio might be a better predictor of stock gains than the price/earnings ratio, as discussed in Chapter 21, but the P/E is plenty useful for screening for underpriced stocks just the same.

Fifth, because many of these guru screens were developed using simple back testing, some report eye-popping past returns. Don't develop false expectations based on those returns.

All that said, the best guru screens are created by people who freely acknowledge these caveats and who take great care to infer investment styles from investment guides, biographies, published letters, and interviews. AAII.com and Validea.com are excellent resources for these screens. Validea is best for someone who just wants to generate a list of stocks, or who wants to plug in a stock symbol to see which gurus would theoretically approve of it. AAII is good for tinkerers, because it gives a write-up detailing what each screen looks for and why. Let's look at some gurus and some clues that are commonly associated with them.

Warren Buffet

Warren Buffet isn't just an investor, he's a brand. His name appears on countless investment guides and financial products, despite him not having written or created them. Many of the things we know about Buffet's investment style do us little good for purposes of building stock screens. For example, he favors concentrated positions in companies he has carefully researched, and he sometimes holds stocks for decades. But some items turn up more than others on Buffet-style stock screens.

- *Favor businesses you can understand.* That might not be a clue you can screen for, unless you choose to eliminate from your searches entire industries you don't understand.
- *Look for a long history of positive operating profits.* Five years or longer is best.
- *Make sure the company resources are generating ample profits.* Rather than focus entirely on earnings and earnings growth, look for companies with high returns on equity—at least 15 percent.
- *Look for shares that are cheap relative to real cash earnings.* You can accomplish this by looking for low price/free-cash-flow ratios.

- *Be sure companies are turning the profits they hang onto into profits for shareholders in the form of higher stock prices.* You'll need a screener with a formula builder and a full list of company financials to do this. Compare retained earnings with share price growth. Look for share price growth that has exceeded retained earnings growth over the last several years.

Peter Lynch

Finding Peter Lynch's stock picking habits is easy. He wrote one of the best-selling books of all time on the subject: *One Up on Wall Street.* But the book wasn't written with stock screening in mind, so not all of the advice it offers will help you build screens. Also, Lynch divides companies into six categories, such as stalwarts, turnarounds, and fast growers, and gives different promising signs to look for in each. He notes that small, fast-growing companies are among his favorites, though, so let's focus on those.

Compare a company's price/earnings ratio with its earnings growth rate. In other words, use the PEG ratio. Keep two things in mind, though. Most stock screeners use PEGs based on forward estimates. Lynch advised comparing trailing P/E ratios with past earnings growth. Also, he adds dividend yields to the earnings growth rate on the bottom side of the ratio. In other words, a company with a trailing P/E of 15 that has grown earnings by 10 percent a year over the past several years and has a dividend yield of 2 percent has a modified PEG ratio of 15/(10 + 2), or 1.25. Lynch favors PEGs between 0.5 and 1.0. You can build this clue using a stock screener with a formula builder.

- *Look for earnings growth that's fast but not too fast.* Growth rates that are too high might not be sustainable for long. Favor companies that are growing earnings at between 20 percent and 50 percent a year.
- *Look for small companies.*
- *Look for relatively undiscovered companies.* You can do this by searching for low levels of institutional ownership, which shows that investment funds and the like haven't yet caught on to the stock. You can also look for stocks that are covered by no more than a few Wall Street analysts.

- *Look for insider buying.*
- *Look for manageable debt levels.* Favor debt/capital ratios that are below their industry averages.

William O'Neill

Unlike Buffet and Lynch, William O'Neill isn't a money manager. He's the founder of a financial newspaper called *Investor's Business Daily*, known for its emphasis on stock charts and *technical analysis*—using past stock movements to predict future ones. O'Neill is also the creator of a popular investment strategy with one of the most awkward acronyms you're likely to hear: CAN SLIM. Most money managers favor value-style investing (it gives them more time to find good stocks). O'Neill's strategy offers an example of a growth and momentum screen. Let's make our way through that acronym, taken from O'Neill's book, *How to Make Money in Stocks.*

C: *Current quarterly earnings per share.* Look for companies with positive operating earnings in their most recent quarter and with recent quarterly earnings growth of at least 20 percent.

A: *Annual earnings increases.* Look for companies that have grown their earnings by at least 25 percent a year over the past five years.

N: *New products, new management, new highs.* The first two items aren't things you can screen for. The third is. Look for companies trading within 5 percent of their 52-week highs, just as we did in the Buy High, Sell Higher screen in Chapter 12.

S: *Supply and demand.* Stocks with fewer shares available to buy tend to move up faster when investors go after them. (Be aware that they tend to move down faster when they're sold, too.) Look for stocks with public floats of less than 20 million shares.

L: *Leader or laggard.* Prefer stocks that have performed better than average. Look for "relative strength" of 70 percent or higher over the past year, which is another way of saying look for stocks that have performed better than 70 percent of the entire market.

I: *Institutional sponsorship.* O'Neill suggests looking for stocks with some, but not too much, ownership by institutions. Look for institutional ownership of between 5 percent and 50 percent of outstanding shares.

M: *Market direction.* This is another thing you can't quite build into your screen. O'Neill recommends not buying stocks when the market looks likely to fall. He offers several ways for determining such a thing, including looking for heavy trading volume with no upward movement in the market. Note that O'Neill is far more concerned with short-term price and market movements than, say, Buffett.

Martin Zweig

Martin Zweig wrote a newsletter, *The Zweig Forecast*, between 1971 and 1998 that was ranked number 1 for risk-adjusted returns by *Hulbert Financial Digest* over the 15 years it covered. He made regular appearances on *Wall Street Week With Louis Rukeyser*, a television program, and famously predicted the stock market crash of 1987. Investors who followed his advice the day of the crash made 9 percent, while those who followed the broad market lost 22 percent. Zweig has always emphasized avoiding losses as much as capturing gains, and not fighting the direction of the market. "If you buy aggressively into a bear market or into individual stocks that are performing badly, it is akin to trying to catch a falling safe," he wrote in his 1986 book *Winning on Wall Street*.

Zweig entered the mutual fund business in 1986. He raised more than $4 billion in eight funds before selling them to another fund company in 1998. Today Zweig manages a handful of hedge funds and serves as asset-allocation strategist for two of the mutual funds he sold. They're both *closed-end funds*, which means they're closed portfolios that trade like stocks. (Most mutual funds are *open-end*, which means they continuously accept new money into the portfolio and can only be bought or sold once a day, at that day's closing price. Open-end funds are priced according to the value of the investments they hold. Closed-end ones are priced according to investor supply and demand at that moment.)

Here's where I'm supposed to cite Zweig's amazing performance record. Only it's not so amazing. As of mid-March, the two closed-end funds had suffered share price declines of 30 percent and 46 percent over the past 10 years, versus an 81 percent increase for the S&P 500 index. (All exclude dividends.) Zweig's hedge fund company says it doesn't disclose returns, as is the choice of all hedge funds.

Of course, I've included Zweig for a reason. The guru screens have vastly outperformed the guru of late. In fact, Zweig-themed screens (say that a few times fast) have produced astounding performance numbers on both Validea.com and AAII.com. According to Validea, as of mid-March its Zweig screen had returned 155 percent since its inception date in July 2003, or about triple the S&P 500 index's return. According to AAII, its Zweig screen produced a 21-fold gain between 1998 and 2007 (the first several years of results are from back testing).

Why are the screens doing so much better than the Zweig funds? The funds hold a mix of stocks and bonds, while the strategies focus on just stocks. But the hurdles facing all mutual funds that we covered in Chapter 4 also hurt returns. The funds hold dozens of stocks each, while the screens settle on just a handful. The screens can target companies that are too small for the funds to buy a meaningful stake in. And of course, the funds have to take out for management fees. Let's look at some of the screen criteria.

- *Look for consistent quarterly earnings growth.* Compare each of the past four quarters with the same quarters a year earlier and make sure earnings are growing.
- *Check for strong annual earnings growth.* Require that earnings over the past three years have increased at least 15 percent a year, on average.
- *Be sure sales are growing, too.* Look for yearly growth of greater than 15 percent over the past three years.
- *Look for accelerating sales growth.* You can do this by requiring that most-recent-quarter growth rates exceed past-year ones, and that past-year ones exceed past-three-year ones.
- *Look for accelerating earnings growth in the same way you looked for accelerating sales growth.*
- *Favor price/earnings ratios that are neither too high nor too low.* Eliminate those that are more than one and a half times their industry median and those that are below 5.

Beyond these criteria you can search for recent share price momentum, insider buying, manageable debt levels, and adequate average trading volume.

Part Four

YOUR NEXT GREAT STOCK, REVISITED

Chapter 24

Which Screen Survivors to Buy

You've run the screen of your choice. You've reduced a database of thousands of companies to just 12 or so companies. And because you've based your screen on a reliable strategy, you're confident that your screen survivors are good stocks. If you were to buy all of them and hold them for a long time, you're pretty sure they'd outperform the broad market.

A couple of them, though, are likely *great* stocks. Although your basket of screen survivors might be expected to outperform the market by several percentage points a year, one or two of those stocks could be the big gainers we discussed in the beginning of the book—the ones that produce returns large enough to more than make up for your mistakes. You've identified the best 12 stocks among thousands. How do you identify the best one or two among the 12?

There are dozens of different directions in which you could take your research at this point. I'll try to organize them into a three-step strategy that makes the most of your time.

The first step is to look for deal breakers. These are signs of problem companies. Since you wouldn't invest in companies that display these signs, there's no point in looking into such companies. You might as well cut them now.

The second step is to get to know your remaining screen survivors. Up until this point your research has focused on measurable facts—on quantities. It's time to look at qualities. Stock screeners aren't good with those. Software can't tell you whether a popular new category of soft drink is a passing fad or whether it's likely to sell well for decades. That big brain of yours that threatened to get in the way during the screening phase is perfect for this sort of work.

The third step is to try to talk yourself out of buying the remaining stocks on your list one by one. You'll look for signs that these companies aren't strong, growing, cheap, or well-managed, and you'll look for other problems that could keep their share prices from rising. If there are any stocks left when you're done, buy them.

Deal Breakers

You've probably already screened away some of these items. Now's the time to look for ones that slipped through.

First, look at the stock's chart. I don't recommend you get too carried away in using stock chart patterns to predict future share price movements, but stock charts are great for spotting potential deal breakers. If the stock price has fallen over the past year, was there a day or couple of days when it suddenly plummeted? If so, you should look through past news items on the stock to see what happened on those days. Something like an earnings miss is no reason to discard the stock. Things like fraud, delays in reporting earnings, major restatements of past earnings, and trouble paying creditors probably mean your research time is better spent with other stocks.

There's an investor for every stock, of course. So-called *distressed equity* investors love nothing better than to work the numbers on companies that are having trouble paying their bills in hopes of finding bargains. But you're not looking for troubled companies that are going to turn things around. You're looking for great companies whose shares are cheaper than they should be.

Pay attention to recent share price momentum, too. If the stock has fallen over the past year, was it still moving lower each day over the past week? If so, consider discarding it or at least setting it aside for now. Price momentum really does tend to predict future stock movements. There's a chance you might identify a bargain stock at what will turn out to be at its lowest trading price for the year, but the odds are better that a falling stock will head lower after you buy it. Better to wait until it has stabilized or even risen a bit and pay the higher price.

If the share price has risen lately, was there a point where it jumped, after which it has traded more or less in a flat line? If so, check the headlines on the stock. That's the chart of a company in the final stages of being bought out by another company. There's little reason for you to buy a stock today if you're going to get cash or shares of another company for your shares a few weeks from now.

Unmanageable debt is a deal breaker, but there's a difference between debt that's unmanageable and debt that's merely large. At this point you need a quick test, not a thorough evaluation. Use a debt/equity or debt/capital cutoff if you know which levels are acceptable for the company's industry. (Heaps of leverage may be fine in one business but a warning sign in another.) Better yet, compare debt with a year's worth of earnings. Use net income before extraordinary items, but add interest expense back in. (There's no point in judging a company's ability to pay its interest after it has already paid its interest.) Look for debt levels that are less than half of a year's worth of income. If you carried debt, not counting your mortgage, equal to more than half your take-home pay, you'd probably find it burdensome. The same goes for companies. Financial companies and companies with big financing divisions sometimes have different rules, since carrying debt is a big part of their business.

It's a good sign for a company when insiders and institutional investors own shares. But when they own too many it could be a sign that management is too entrenched or that there are few big buyers left to attract big sellers that might materialize. Consider pitching stocks with more than three-quarters of outstanding shares owned by insiders and institutions.

Low trading volume might be a problem. It means a stock probably won't attract institutional buyers. Also, it means a big sell order could send the stock sliding. Think about disregarding stocks that trade less than, say, $1 million worth of shares on an average day.

Get to Know Your Screen Survivors

It's time to learn everything you can about the business you're thinking about buying your way into. Financial Web sites often publish company descriptions on their stock quote pages, but I want you to ignore those. Companies themselves often have an "About Us" page on their Web sites. Those are more helpful, but you can do better. Pull up a copy of the company's most recent 10-K filing. Either access it yourself through Edgar or go through a finance Web site whose stock quote pages provide links to SEC filings.

The 10-K provides perhaps the best description you'll find of a company's business. It helps you to avoid a problem that has reached epidemic levels among corporate marketing departments. I call it the *solutions problem*. I'm not sure exactly when or why it happened, but companies have taken to describing themselves as esoteric solutions providers rather than simply explaining what they make or do in exchange for money. That's especially true of those short self-descriptions they post on their Web sites, which are often identical to those posted on financial Web sites. A company that makes routers and switches for computer networks suddenly provides communications solutions, and one that makes airplane innards now provides aerospace solutions. I'm waiting for Nathan's to start saying it provides hot dog solutions.

The business descriptions in 10-K filings are generally clearer, far more complete and less sales-y than those you see elsewhere. That's because companies can and will be sued if they're not. Litigious investors who lose money in stocks often target those companies for lawsuits, saying the companies didn't make them fully aware of potential problems and weaknesses. And they don't just go after the companies. They target the individuals who run those companies. Reading a 10-K, then, is like interviewing management with a team of lawyers standing behind you just waiting for them to exaggerate or withhold an important fact.

For that reason, the company descriptions in 10-K filings read more like confessionals than investment pitches. A company that manages prescription drug plans will tell you straightaway that three-quarters of its sales come from Medicare and Medicaid (in the United States, taxpayer-funded health plans for the old and poor, respectively), and that sales could dry up if Congress decides to change the reimbursement rates. An oil shipper will tell you that its ships are old by industry standards and might need replacing soon. A software maker will tell you its most popular title might violate a competitor's patent, and that hearings are underway.

Read the company history and the growth strategy. Pay attention to which companies your company competes with, and why it thinks it has an advantage over them. This is likely the fairest explanation you'll find. Also, look for a breakdown of where sales come from. Too great of a reliance on one customer is a big risk. You should be given an idea of the overall size of your company's market and what share of that market it holds. Depending on what your company does for money, you may be given a demographic description of its average customer.

You'll likely see a long list of risk factors. Don't be put off by how many of them there are. This is where companies try to foresee every possible way they could fail and tell you about it, so that you can't say you weren't warned. Some of these factors are generic. Just about every company says its business could suffer if the economy tanks, if it fails to implement its business plan, if it loses a lawsuit, or if it can't keep up with a competitor. By now you should have an idea of how management is controlling the risk factors that can be controlled.

We'll check back with the 10-K for the financial tables in a moment. For now, head to the company's Web site. In the investor relations part of the site, look for information on corporate governance. You can read bios on the people who run the company if you like, but pay particular attention to the relationship between board members (also called directors) and managers (also called executives). If the chief executive officer is also the founder of the company, that's a plus. Founder-run companies tend to outperform the broad market. One study found they did so by eight percentage points a year over the 10 years ended 2002. If board members are also managers, that's generally a negative sign. The job of the board is to make sure management is taking care of the shareholders.

To best do that, it should be independent. (The larger the company, the less of an excuse it has for not hiring an independent board.)

Sometimes the company's Web site has presentations that have been prepared for analyst meetings. If so, take a look. Keep in mind that these are sales pitches, but they often contain a further articulation of the business plan and of competitive advantages. You might find an archived audio file of the company's most recent quarterly results announcement. If so, have a listen. Most of the first part will consist of the chief financial officer reading the financial tables. You can do that yourself. The last bit, though, often has management fielding questions from analysts. These answers might be useful.

If you have access to analyst reports, read them over. If you have access to recent news stories from business publications, read them, too. You're not looking for someone to advise you on whether to buy the stock. You'll figure that out on your own. But analysts and journalists may have uncovered facts you haven't. If the company has products or services that you can sample where you live, by all means try them out, but save this step for last. You might as well learn everything you can from your desk in order to make the most of your time.

Talk Yourself Out of It

You now have an even smaller basket of good stocks. None of them have deal-breaking attributes. You're familiar with each company's business, products, market, and risks. It's time to talk yourself out of buying shares if you can. You're not looking for perfection, of course. You're looking for all the characteristics of great stocks: shares are cheap, and they come from companies that are growing, strong, and well managed. If your remaining companies don't compare favorably on any of these points, they're not worth buying.

Cheap and Growing

Start with cheap and growing. You'll want to consider them at the same time because they relate to each other. A cheap stock, after all, is one that's priced lower than its growth prospects warrant.

Pull up that 10-K filing again. Financial Web sites often list only three years' worth of this information, while 10-K filings usually list five or more. The extra years give you a better feel for long-term company trends. You can look up three-year and five-year sales growth rates on Web sites, too. But looking at the individual years gives you a better sense of the degree to which sales growth is slowing. Calculate sales growth rates for each of the past few years. Then look at the growth rates for manufacturing and corporate costs. Sales should be growing faster than costs, or the company isn't taking advantage of its increasing scale.

Calculate earnings growth rates, and then earnings per share growth rates. Earnings should be growing as fast as or faster than sales. If they're not, the company might be cutting prices in order to ring the register more. Earnings per share should be growing as fast as or faster than earnings. If they're not, the company may be issuing shares too freely to raise money or to reward employees.

Look for any years that earnings were negative or sharply lower. If you see any, look into what happened those years. (Past 10-K filings should tell you.) Sometimes a company has a year of negative earnings due to *big-bath* charges. That happens when management decides to erase all of its past mistakes at once with a series of asset write-downs and restructuring charges. It's like a kid who, after getting caught breaking your window, admits to denting your car with a football, too. There's no sense in having you get mad twice. Big-bath charges from a few years ago shouldn't affect today's stock price, but they're a sign of past failures. If broad conditions like competition from imports or difficult relations with labor caused those failures once, they could easily do so again. If management caused the failures, they should have since been replaced.

Now take a look at sales and earnings per share estimates for this fiscal year and next. You'll find those on financial Web sites, not on SEC filings. Calculate the percent growth those estimates represent. Consider how those numbers compare with the past growth rates you've just looked at. Next, look at the company's history over the past four quarters of hitting its earnings targets. If it consistently misses them, the remaining estimates might not be credible. Now look at the long-term earnings per share growth forecast. That's the annual rate at which analysts figure the company will increase its earnings over the next several years, recall. You should have a good idea by now of whether this figure is credible. If it's not, discount it. If a company has grown its earnings by 14 percent, 13 percent, and 12 percent in each of its past three years and the long-term projection stands at 20 percent, you're probably better off using 10 percent in your assumptions, unless you have a strong reason to believe the company's earnings are set to jump.

Estimates will only help you for companies that have both earnings and analyst coverage, of course. If you're new to analyzing stocks on your own, you should stick to companies that have both. If you're not, you can use past sales and earnings growth to gauge a company's trajectory, or past sales and expense growth to judge when it will turn a profit.

You should have a credible long-term earnings growth projection at this point. Compare it with the stock's price/earnings ratio based on this year's earnings forecast. Think carefully about buying a stock whose P/E ratio is more than one and a half times its long-term EPS growth forecast (PEG greater than 1.5, in other words). Chances are, there are better bargains available to you.

Strong

Good companies benefit from a virtuous circle. Companies that are growing their sales and earnings in a balanced fashion and that are well-managed (which we'll check for in a moment) tend to make good decisions in other parts of their business, too. They tend to borrow responsibly, and to qualify for favorable interest rates when they do. They tend to generate cash and to have enough of it in the till to fund their operations comfortably.

Have a good look at several years' worth of a company's cash flow statements for other signs of strength. Recall that there are three sections that show cash generated from operating, investing, and financing. Strong businesses have generally positive cash flows from operations. They don't just produce paper earnings; they bring in cash. Cash flows from investing activities will probably be mostly negative. That's because they reflect the money companies spend on capital investments like plants and equipment and also on buying other companies. But study the relationship between cash flows from operations and investing activities with several years' worth of results side by side. A company that can pay for its expansion by generating cash from operations is likely a strong company.

Assuming you're not researching a young, barely profitable company, look for more operating cash coming in than investing cash going out. Combine operating cash flow and investing cash flow into a net figure. If it consistently falls short of the net income reported at the top of the statement, be wary. That's a sign of a company that consistently benefits from accounting rules, and not necessarily from cash coming in.

Check the cash from financing activity, the last of the three sections of the cash flow statement. A record of consistently positive numbers might be a problem. It could mean the company relies too heavily on borrowing and issuing new shares to raise funds. That won't help increase the stock price.

Well Managed

Good managers consistently find lucrative ways to invest your money. If they have more money on their hands than they have attractive projects for investment, they send the extra back to you through dividends and share repurchases. Calculate your company's *returns on invested capital* (ROIC) from each of the past few years. Here's one way to do that: First, determine the company's tax rate. To do that, look at the income statement and divide income tax by pretax income. So if the company had pretax income of $400 and it paid $100 in taxes, its tax rate is 25 percent. If a company is paying a negligible amount in taxes, it's probably benefiting from temporary tax breaks. You want to judge performance without any special benefits, so use a minimum rate of 25 percent or so. Next, apply the tax rate to operating income. If operating income is $800 and the tax rate is 25 percent, you should end up with $600. That figure is the company's aftertax operating profit. It ignores noncash adjustments and items that aren't related to current operations. You'll use it for the top side of the ROIC ratio.

Now, the bottom side: Turn to the balance sheet. Subtract short-term debt from current liabilities. Then subtract the figure you end up with from total assets. This is the figure to use for invested capital. If you want to be as accurate as possible, calculate this figure for each quarter during the year and take the average of the four values.

Divide the first figure by the second. That's the company's ROIC. Note that there are a near-endless number of variations on how you can calculate ROIC, which is probably why many stock screeners don't include the figure. As you become more familiar with company financial statements, you may want to make adjustments to the formula for each company, depending on what you view as important to its earnings and its capital resources.

Calculate ROIC for each of the past few years and for the company's most recent quarter. Are the returns healthy? Standard finance theory says that a company's returns on invested capital should be higher than its *weighted average cost of capital* (WACC), a combination of the interest it pays on debt and the return stock investors theoretically demand on their capital. Calculating the latter is tricky, because the formula depends in part on using a measure of risk, and we've already seen that that's more problematic than finance formulas suggest. The average WACC for large, established companies is between 9 percent and 12 percent. A ROIC of 15 percent or higher is a good sign. Notice whether the figure is rising or falling each year. Companies find it increasingly difficult to maintain high internal returns as they mature unless they have strong advantages that keep competitors from cutting into their pricing power. A high, stable ROIC is one of the best signs that you've found a great stock.

Have you talked yourself out of investing in most of your screen survivors? Maybe they weren't growing fast enough to make up for their price/earnings ratios, maybe they were producing more paper profits than cash profits, and maybe their internal returns weren't high enough. If you have one or two stocks left, the chances are high that they're great ones. Do some hands-on research, if you can. Visit retailers, eat at restaurants, and so on. If the company sells mainly to other companies or professionals, try to find a customer to talk to. For a maker of construction products, for example, talk to a building contractor. Learn as much as you can about competing services and products and what keeps the ones your company sells in demand. When you're convinced this is a business you want to own, buy shares.

Now all you have to do is figure out when it's time to sell. Hopefully that's a long, long time away.

Chapter 25

When to Sell

Knowing when to sell stocks is second only to knowing how to find great stocks in terms of its importance to growing your stash of money. Yet investment books often devote many pages to finding stocks but leave only a skimpy section on how to sell them.

This book will follow in that tradition. Don't blame me. Throughout the book, I've tried to take stock-picking ideas developed by meticulous researchers and incorporate those ideas into stock screens. I'd love to do the same here. But it turns out that while there's plenty of good research available on finding stocks, there's little available on selling them. How can I be expected to steal something that doesn't exist?

Short of being able to offer selling tips that are firmly based in evidence, and not wanting to simply whip a few of them up as an afterthought, I'll present here the ideas I hear most often on the subject from investors and market strategists.

Some investors make selling decisions easy on themselves by using an automated, mathematical approach. For example, an investor might decide to limit losses by selling stocks immediately when they fall 8 percent from their purchase price. Since growth stocks can often produce price fluctuations larger than 8 percent on their way up, these investors might allow for a bigger decline on rising stocks—say, 20 percent. Often they'll use *stop orders,* which are stock trades that get sent automatically once a stock trades at a certain price. By continuously ratcheting up their stop orders to keep them 20 percent below the stock's current trading price, these investors make selling something that takes care of itself.

Such strategies, despite making limited use of the price momentum effect, don't seem ideal for long-term investors. By using an automated system, you'll run a constant risk of being sold out of a stock that has merely dipped on its way to new heights. That seems something of a pessimistic approach to deciding when to sell what you believe to be great stocks. We've focused mainly on company fundamentals—earnings and such—when finding great stocks, so maybe it's best to focus on fundamentals when deciding when to sell them.

Decide up front whether you've invested in a growth stock or a value stock—that is, a popular stock or an unpopular one. Review the section on growth and value stocks in Chapter 11 if you're unsure of the difference. You buy these stocks for different reasons, so it makes sense to sell them for different reasons.

You buy growth stocks because of their rapid increases in sales and earnings, even if you have to pay more for these stocks. Watch earnings reports carefully for signs that sales and earnings are slowing sharply. Also, watch for missed earnings estimates. But be careful not to sell these stocks merely because their price/earnings ratios have gotten high. They're supposed to be high. It's a sign of popularity. Always compare price/earnings ratios with earnings growth rates. Essentially, you buy growth stocks because they're already doing things that make investors happy. Sell them when they start to disappoint.

You buy value stocks because they're cheap, even though they're imperfect. Be more lenient with these stocks when it comes to things like missed earnings estimates, as long as there are broad signs that the companies are making progress in turning things around in order to fetch higher P/E ratios for their shares. But be wary when those P/E ratios approach or exceed industry averages. You buy value stocks because they're making investors unhappy, which has made their share prices cheap. Sell them when they start to make investors too happy.

The following signs are reasons to rethink holding either a growth or value stock:

- A management team that doesn't own many shares itself regularly issues new shares.
- A cash buildup is combined with no word from management on how the money is to be spent.
- The company purchases a big company—one worth, say, more than a quarter the value of the acquiring company. This isn't necessarily a bad sign, but it means you now own a different company. Make sure it's a company you like.
- Managers are evasive when it comes time to discuss mistakes or problems.
- A major earnings restatement for past periods doesn't come with a major firing of the managers responsible.
- One-time accounting charges, contrary to what the name implies, begin to turn up each quarter.
- Profit margins, returns on invested capital, or, in the case of retailers, same-store sales deteriorate. (Same-store sales ignore sales increases that come from newly opened or acquired stores, so they give a good idea of whether each store, on average, is doing better or worse. Be particularly cautious of retailers that are adding new stores while same-store sales aren't growing.)

Take taxes into consideration when selling stocks only if you happen to be approaching the one-year anniversary of buying them. That's the current cutoff between paying higher taxes on short-term gains or lower taxes on long-term gains. Make taxes part of your decision, but not the driving force behind it. Your goal is to maximize your aftertax returns, not to minimize your taxes.

Read each quarterly financial report, both the press release you'll find under the company news sections on financial Web sites and the full filing from the Edgar database. Calculate the numbers you need (profit margins, return ratios, growth rates) yourself, rather than relying on financial Web sites to get them right. Often, that will make you aware of something you wouldn't otherwise have picked up on, like that sales growth for the quarter was impressive but that most of it came from acquisitions, not from improvements in the existing business.

Above all, don't sell stocks merely because they've gone up. Make your decisions based on fundamental attributes, such as valuation, growth rates, efficiency, and financial strength. That's difficult to do in practice. It's exciting when stocks go up. It's tempting to want to lock in those gains before something goes wrong, even when the numbers suggest you should hang on and let great stocks do what they're supposed to do over long time periods. Here's hoping you face countless such dilemmas.

Index